# Upgrade your English Essay

Tony Myers

FORMERLY AT THE UNIVERSITY OF STIRLING

ARNOLD

A member of the
Hodder Headline Group
LONDON
Co-published in the United States of America by
Oxford University Press Inc., New York

First published in Great Britain in 2002 by
Arnold, a member of the Hodder Headline Group,
338 Euston Road, London NW1 3BH

**http://www.arnoldpublishers.com**

Co-published in the United States of America by
Oxford University Press Inc.,
198 Madison Avenue, New York, NY10016

*British Library Cataloguing in Publication Data*
A catalogue record for this book is available from the British Library

*Library of Congress Cataloging-in-Publication Data*
A catalog record for this book is available from the Library of Congress

ISBN 0 340 80791 1

1 2 3 4 5 6 7 8 9 10

Production Editor: Rada Radojicic
Production Controller: Martin Kerans
Cover Design: Terry Griffiths

Typeset in 10/12 pt Formata by Cambrian Typesetters, Frimley, Surrey
Printed and bound in Malta by Gutenberg Press

What do you think about this book? Or any other Arnold title?
Please send your comments to feedback.arnold@hodder.co.uk

# Upgrade your
# English Essay

*Other titles in this series*

**Upgrade your Spanish**    Abigail Lee Six
                           ISBN 0 340 76186 5
**Upgrade your French**     Margaret Jubb
                           ISBN 0 340 76345 0
**Upgrade your German**     Annemarie Künzl-Snodgrass and Silke Mentchen
                           ISBN 0 340 806621

# Contents

# Acknowledgements

My first thanks go to Elena Seymenliyska for her help and encouragement in completing this project. I am also grateful to my colleagues and students at the University of Stirling for their assistance in honing the techniques discussed in the book. And finally I would like to record my deep indebtedness to Ali for support *in excelsis*.

*Tony Myers*

# Introduction

The aim of this book is to provide A-Level students and first-year undergraduates with a practical guide to writing better English essays. In tandem with the other guides in the *Upgrade* series, this book will help you to improve your results by at least one grade. So, if you currently expect to get a B grade in your essay, this book will help you to get an A. Or if you keep getting Cs and Ds, follow the advice in these pages to get a much better result next time.

**This book will improve your essay by at least one grade.**

Each chapter of *Upgrade your English* has two objectives in mind. First, it details and explains the key concepts your teachers expect you to know and the examiners are looking for in your essay. Second, it shows you how to apply these concepts at a practical level, supplying you with a summary of questions at the end of each chapter which you can then apply directly next time you have to write an essay.

**It explains the key concepts you should know and shows you how to apply them.**

*Upgrade your English* can be used in two different ways: it will help you improve both *exam* and *coursework* essays. So if you are revising for exams, you can use this book as part of your revision programme and it will provide you with core information on key topics in a systematic and reassuring progression. At the same time, if you are completing coursework, you'll find that the different elements of the essay-writing process have been grouped together, allowing you to dip in and out of the book for easy and quick reference. So should you, for example, be writing an analysis of Wordsworth, you can stay focused and go straight to the chapters on poetry, rather than having to read interesting but not directly relevant details about Hardy's novels.

**It will help you improve both coursework and exam essays.**

In addition, *Upgrade your English* is split into three sections. Each of these sections explains a central aspect of writing better English essays:

1  **Essay writing** This section offers tips and advice on assembling the structure of a good essay. It shows how to answer a question, how to create a convincing argument and what teachers and examining boards expect to find in a well-written answer.
2  **Technical language** This section explains what should constitute the general content of a good essay. It demonstrates how to analyse the different types of literary language and form, and it shows you how to apply the technical concepts and idioms of analysis.

3    **Genre** This section is devoted to an analysis of the three main genres: drama, poetry and the novel. In each case, you will be shown both how to recognise the specific elements of the genre and how to write about them.

Throughout the three sections, techniques and concepts are illustrated by examples taken from all of the major set texts you are studying, together with individual chapters on the most frequently examined areas. Each chapter will also employ specimen questions, offering pragmatic advice on the best and worst ways of answering them.

**Illustrated throughout by examples from set texts and specimen questions.**

In short, *Upgrade your English Essay* is an essential supplement to your course texts which will harness your existing abilities, hone your skills and ultimately help you *improve your essay grades*.

# SECTION 1

# Essay writing

# Answering the question

*Have you ever written the most brilliant, well-researched essay you could think of and then found at the end of it that you forgot to answer the question? It sounds obvious, I know, but too many students' essays are doomed to fail long before they have even been finished. Whatever great thoughts you might have in your head when planning an essay, they mean nothing to your teachers: they have in front of them only what you've written and if that doesn't answer the question, your essay doesn't get a grade. It's as simple as that.*

## WHAT'S INVOLVED IN ANSWERING A QUESTION?

Answering a question involves two connected processes.

- First, you *must respond to the terms of the question*. This is the planning stage. It is where you decide how to answer a question either in your head or on rough paper. For example, if you were set the question, 'Discuss the meaning of the darkness in Joseph Conrad's *Heart of Darkness*', you would have to decide what the darkness is. You would have to determine whether to write about the literal or the metaphorical darkness, whether to interpret the darkness as ambiguous, whether to include a discussion of the dark tone of the novel or to concentrate on the imagery of darkness, and so on.

- Secondly, *you must show that you are responding to the terms of the question*. This is the writing stage. It is where you compose the essay that your teacher will mark. If you were answering the question on Conrad's *Heart of Darkness*, for example, you would have to compose an answer that solely focused on a discussion of the meaning of the darkness in the novel. This means you would have to define the darkness, explain what it means and analyse it *throughout* your essay.

Of the two steps here, the second one initially seems the most important. After all, if you can't show that you are answering the question in your essay, how is the person marking it supposed to know that you have responded properly to the question? However, what's crucial to remember here is that the planning and the writing are related and the planning always comes first. Even if you only plan essays in your head, it is at this stage that you set the agenda for the rest of the essay-writing process. If you're not convinced about this, ask yourself the following question: how many times have you decided what an essay is about, only to change your mind half way through actually writing it? The chances are that once you've committed yourself to a certain answer, only dynamite will make you change your mind. The trick, then, is to get the agenda right from the beginning.

**Remember that if you plan it right, you write it right.**

To help you with this, follow these four steps:

1   Identify the terms of the question.
2   Define the terms of the question.
3   Use these definitions as a prism to look at the text.
4   Write your essay by using what you see through the prism.

### Step 1: Identify the terms of the question

First of all, you have to know what exactly is meant by 'the terms of the question'. Basically, the terms of the question are its *key words*, the words other than those doing the questioning or which are merely pronouns or articles. Just to be sure you can do it, pick out the terms of the question in these real examples:

**1)** Discuss the ways in which Beloved in Toni Morrison's *Beloved*, is both a personal and public ghost.

**2)** How far do you agree that Shakespeare's main concern in *Richard II* is to explore different kinds of kingship?

**3)** 'It is essential to an understanding of Emily Brontë's *Wuthering Heights* that we read it as a gothic novel.' Discuss.

Answers: **1)** Beloved, personal, public, ghost; **2)** main, kingship; **3)** essential, gothic. If you missed out 'main' and 'essential' here, it is worth remembering that adjectives such as these not only qualify the question, but should qualify your answer as well.

The terms of a question, then, are a signpost to the right answer. They direct you along a specific analytical path, guiding you on the way that – for best results – the essay should be answered. So make the question work for you – use its key terms to steer you in the right direction.

## Step 2: Define the terms of the question

Your first step in answering a question and one of the best ways to demonstrate that you are responding to the terms of a question, is to define those terms. Let me be clear here. This doesn't just apply to difficult or obscure terms but to apparently clear-cut words too. You may think that **Always define your terms.**
the meaning of a word is obvious, but you shouldn't make the mistake of assuming it's obvious to the people who are marking your essays.

Let me give you an example of a word that crops up at least once in almost every exam paper: 'conflict'.

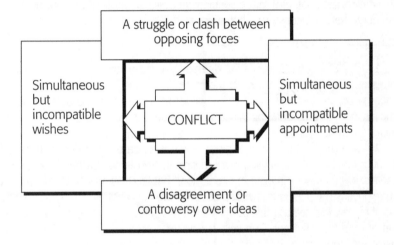

Here are four of the many different meanings for the word 'conflict'. They all overlap each other, but there are also subtle differences between them. Two are concerned with *actions*, while two are concerned with *thoughts*. Two centre upon *incompatibilities*, while two refer to *actual clashes*. Whichever meaning or meanings you chose would affect not only the parts of the text you wrote about, but also the ultimate direction of your essay.

Of course, the easiest way to find out the different meanings of a word is to consult a dictionary. As a general rule, the bigger the dictionary the better it is, and the more definitions you will have to choose from. In my opinion, the *Oxford English Dictionary* and the *Collins English Dictionary* are two of the best.

Once you've located the definitions in the dictionary, you have two choices. You can either quote from it directly, or rephrase the definitions in your own words. If you quote from it directly you can be sure of pin-point accuracy. If you rephrase the definition in your own words you can be sure you have understood its meaning.

The crucial factor here, however, is that you define the terms of the question.

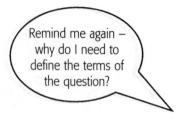

Remind me again –
why do I need to
define the terms of
the question?

There are three main reasons:

1   It shows you are engaging with the question.
2   It eliminates potential misunderstandings between you and your teachers.
3   It will help you construct a better essay.

Taking these in order:

**1**   By defining the terms of the question you show you are *engaging* with the question. Engaging with a question is preferable to just mentioning it because it means you are involved in an *active* rather than *passive* response to it. Which means that you are not taking things at face value, but analysing them, which, after all, is what writing an essay is all about.

**2**   Defining the terms of the question also eliminates any confusion that might arise between what you think a word means and what your teacher thinks a word means. If you do not eliminate this confusion, your teachers may well think that you have not answered the question because you have not considered its terms from the point of view that seems most obvious to them. If, on the other hand, you provide a set of clear-cut definitions then your teachers will accept them and will mark your essay with these terms in mind rather than their own. This is particularly true if you quote your definitions from a dictionary because they lend a form of authority to what might otherwise be considered a somewhat individual interpretation of words.

**3**   Perhaps the most compelling reason why you should provide a definition of each of the question's main terms is that doing so will help you write a better essay. At a basic level, this is because having spent a fair amount of effort on researching these definitions you will be loath not to use them. And, of course, if you use them you will be going some way to answering the question.

At another level, your definitions will enable you to answer the question you have been set. Faced with a blank piece of paper on one side and the question on the other, with only the text and a shaky pen to guide you, you might be one of those students tempted to thrash about in an agony of hopelessness as you seek for inspiration in everything from the bottom of your coffee cup to the inscrutable

**Your dictionary definitions will help you get started.**

development of your best friend's love life. If you are one of those students, then trust me: these things will not help. You are much better off consulting a good dictionary.

This is because the definitions you have researched are a way into the question. They provide the co-ordinates by which you will be able to map a route through your essay. You will hardly ever be set questions such as 'Discuss *Othello*' or 'Examine *Jude the Obscure*' and there is a very good reason for this. Your teachers know that if they set a question like that most students would suffer from a kind of academic agoraphobia. You would be paralysed by fear at the great open spaces of the text, too daunted by the scale of

**The terms of a question provide you with a focus for your answer.**

the task in front of you to do anything but meander hopelessly across the pages. The reason you are given such questions as 'Discuss the function of jealousy in *Othello*' or 'Examine the role of natural imagery in *Jude the Obscure*' is precisely to stop this happening by providing your essay with a focus.

**Step 3: Use these definitions as a prism to look at the text**
The definitions you look up are a kind of prism through which you can look at the text you are supposed to be writing about. Through this prism you should be able to see only those features of the text that are of relevance to the question. Everything else should fall out of view. It's like a conjuring trick, only it has the advantage that you don't have to be a magician to perform it.

Let me show you what I mean by using an example. Suppose you were given the question 'Discuss the role of blindness in D.H. Lawrence's short story "The Blind Man"'. This is a story about a man who is blind, called Maurice, and his meeting with a man who can see, called Bertie. At first the physically capable but mentally slow Maurice is afraid of the intellectual powers of Bertie, but by the end of the story Maurice has gained the ascendancy and Bertie is left 'like a mollusc whose shell is broken'. The key to this transformation is the concept of blindness.

In my dictionary there are well over thirty definitions of the word. From these we may pick a couple of the more relevant examples. Thus, while 'blindness' refers to a condition of physical sightlessness, it also refers to an inability or unwillingness to understand or discern. If we may attribute the first definition to Maurice, who actually is sightless, it is Bertie who proves to lack the kind of spiritual and sensual understanding which, for the narrator of this story, is a much more disabling blindness.

It is no surprise, then, that while Maurice worries about his appearance – what can be seen – it is Bertie who frets that 'at the centre' – what cannot be seen – 'he felt himself neuter, nothing'. Just to make sure that the reader understands exactly who is the blind man of the title, there are several references at the end of the story which are suggestive of a more physical blindness on Bertie's part, such as his 'sunken eyes' and the fact that they are 'glazed with misery'. The whole story, in other words, plays off the two contrasting definitions of blindness against each other.

In so doing, it affirms the time-honoured point that Bertie seeing, sees not, while Maurice, although blind, has 20/20 spiritual vision, which is not distracted by the superficial aspects of life.

### Step 4: Write your essay by using what you see through the prism

Put your notes on the text you are writing about to one side and, from now on, use only your notes on what you see through the prism of the definitions. Remember, you are answering a question about a specific topic. You should not write a discussion about everything in the novel, play or poem in front of you. Nor are you expected to write about anything you like. Other features of the text might seem more interesting, but if they are not related to the terms of the question, they are irrelevant.

Let me show you what I mean. Here are extracts from two essays answering the question, 'Discuss the role of the oral tradition in Chinua Achebe's *Things Fall Apart'*. Which essay do you think responds best to the terms of the question, A or B?

**Keep your essay focused.**

**A)** The destruction of the oral tradition in Chinua Achebe's *Things Fall Apart* is an example of how African societies were destroyed by the colonial activities of the European empires. The white men are 'locusts' to the native tribes and they destroy not only the oral tradition, but all traditions. What is so terrible about the destruction of the oral tradition, and the other traditions in the novel, is that these traditions held the Igbo tribe together and when they are destroyed, the tribe, like the 'Things' in the title, 'Fall Apart'.

**B)** The oral tradition is very important to the Igbo tribe. It is a means of handing down customs and beliefs from generation to generation by word of mouth. This is why the Igbo are always telling stories and proverbs. They have no books or newspapers. All their history, news and religion is told by word of mouth. Sadly, the Igbo's oral tradition is destroyed by the white men. Because of this, *Things Fall Apart* is a book and not a tale.

Can you see that B is a better essay than A? Although it might sound quite good, essay A does not really engage with the terms of question. It does not focus on 'the role of the oral tradition', but instead uses it as a springboard to launch into a discussion on the destructiveness of the European empires. In other words, the author uses the oral tradition only as an example of something else s/he wants to write about.

Essay B, on the other hand, makes the oral tradition its centre. It defines the oral tradition and then uses this definition as a prism to look in the novel for what is relevant to the question. So even though essay A *mentions* the terms of the question more times than essay B, it does not *engage* with them by defining, explaining or analysing them.

## SUMMARY

If you have followed the advice set out in this chapter so far, then you will already have shown that you have responded to the terms of the question *before* you ever put pen to paper, or finger to keyboard. This is because, as I mentioned earlier, if you plan it right, you write it right. By defining the terms of the question, you have responded to them. These definitions then form the prism through which you look at a text, which in turn forms the basis of your plan and what you write about in your essay. And your essay, of course, is where you are judged to have answered the question or not. If you think of this process as a flow chart, you can see how everything depends upon getting it right from the start.

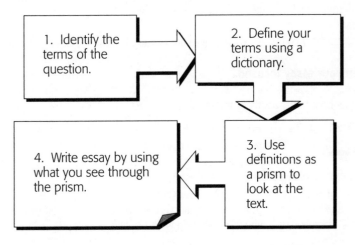

**Always ask yourself:**
✔ Which are the key terms of the question?
✔ What do the key terms of the question mean?
✔ Where and how are the key terms of the question located in the text?

# Constructing an argument

*How often have you written an essay in which you thought you made a series of cunning points only to have it returned to you with the comment that it 'lacks a strong argument'? This disheartening remark does not constitute an invitation to engage your tutor in a terrible quarrel in which gloves are slapped about faces and duelling swords are procured for a battle at dawn. Instead, it is a request for you to assemble all your individual points about a text within one, overall point. This overall point is the argument or thesis of your essay.*

### IF YOU'RE NOT SURE WHAT AN ARGUMENT IS . . .

. . . a quick analogy with the world of law should make it all clear. In a courtroom, one lawyer argues that a defendant is guilty, while another lawyer argues that a defendant is not guilty. The argument therefore concerns the guilt or otherwise of the client. When writing an essay, you are in a similar position to a lawyer making a case for or against a client in which the object is to convince the jury of that client's guilt or innocence.

In a court of law, each lawyer will produce pieces of evidence to support their respective arguments. Thus, in the course of a trial, each side might examine the reliability of witnesses, police statements, alibis, forensic evidence, expert testimony, and so on. These pieces of evidence are what we might consider the points of an essay, each one of which may be tested on its individual merits. However, the only function of these individual pieces of evidence is to support the general argument of each side concerning the guiltiness or otherwise of the defendant. Similarly, when you write an essay, all the points in it should be there to substantiate and corroborate the argument you are advancing about a particular text.

> **All the points you make in an essay are solely there to support your argument.**

The difference between your essay and a court of law is, of course, that a lawyer only constructs an argument about the culpability of a client, whereas you will hardly ever be asked if *Animal Farm* is guilty of murder or if *Far From the Madding Crowd* should be convicted of sheep rustling.

### WHAT CONSTITUTES AN ARGUMENT IN LITERARY CRITICISM?

Quite simply, an argument is a general proposition or idea about a novel, story or poem. For example:

- '*Hamlet* is a play exploring indecisiveness' is an argument.
- '*David Copperfield* is a thinly veiled autobiography of Charles Dickens' is an argument.
- 'Salman Rushdie's *Midnight's Children* undertakes a strong critique of imperialism' is an argument.
- 'Andrew Marvell's poems utilize bizarre and inconsistent imagery' is an argument.
- '*Coronation Street* represents an accurate depiction of working-class life in modern Britain' is an argument.

These statements are all arguments insofar as they are propositions which may be debated and their respective merits supported with evidence.

These arguments, like the ones you are expected to construct, are about one of two subjects: the themes of a text or the techniques used to portray those themes. The themes of a text are the main ideas it examines, either explicitly or implicitly. In this sense a theme is a paraphrase of a text in terms of ideas, summing up what it is about. For example, as most of you have probably discovered, a common theme in Shakespeare's history plays is kingship. A common theme in Shakespeare's comedies is disguise. When you construct an argument, you should try to describe a text in terms of a theme or themes. For example, 'Chaucer's *The Wife of Bath* examines the role of women in medieval society'. The 'role of women' is the theme here. Similarly, 'the effects of slavery' is the theme in the argument 'Toni Morrison's *Beloved* portrays the effects of slavery on African-Americans'.

> **An argument should be about the themes of a text or the techniques used to portray those themes.**

A very good argument will describe a text in terms of a theme *and* link that to the techniques which help portray that theme. So, for example, you might argue that 'Emily Brontë uses an unreliable narrator to highlight the gothic excess of *Wuthering Heights*'. The 'unreliable narrator' is the technique here, and 'gothic' is the theme. Or you might propose that 'Throughout *Candide* Voltaire employs satire in order to critique eighteenth-century French society'. Here, 'satire' is the technique and 'critique' is the theme.

> **A very good argument will propose a link between the themes of a text and the techniques used to portray them.**

### SOME QUESTIONS ARE DESIGNED TO HELP YOU

What you will no doubt have noticed is how very familiar the above arguments look. This is because many essay questions already advance some sort of argument – purely, of course, to make your life easier. How many times have you seen an essay question such as 'Examine the proposition that *King Lear* is a play about good and evil'? Or one like '"Margaret Atwood's *The Handmaid's Tale* is a feminist examination of the exploitation of women." Discuss'? If you have studied English Literature before, the chances are that questions such as these will be like old friends. Invite them in, offer them a drink: they are as good as it gets.

**Many questions already propose an argument with which you must agree or disagree.**

The reason I say this is that all the hard work has been done for you – the argument is stated in the question. All that remains to be done with these type of essays is for you to decide whether or not you agree with the argument being proposed by the question and to produce evidence for or against it accordingly.

There are, however, other types of question which are less friendly because they fail to propose an argument. Questions such as 'Examine the role of the dream in Scott Fitzgerald's *Tender is the Night*' and 'Discuss the different types of love in *A Midsummer Night's Dream*' contain no arguments beyond the implicit claims that these respective texts mention dreams and love. Worse than that, questions like these invite unsuspecting students into a trap. You might well suppose that as there is no general argument in the question, you do not have to invent one yourself, and

**Even if a question does not propose an argument, your essay should still be based on an argument.**

that the question merely bids you to list, for example, the different types of love in *A Midsummer Night's Dream*. If you were tempted to suppose this, you would be wrong: *every essay should be constructed around an argument*.

### HOW DO YOU CONSTRUCT AN ARGUMENT FROM SCRATCH?

Well, first of all, you remember your prime objective: answer the question. So, for example, if we take the question 'Discuss the different types of love in *A Midsummer Night's Dream*' (which is an old favourite that you are certain to encounter sooner or later), your initial engagement with the topic will involve defining 'love'. Having found, unsurprisingly, that 'love' is, among other things, both a verb that means 'to have a great attachment to', and a noun that means 'an intense emotion of affection', you can then proceed to identify instances of these in the play. So far so good, but don't forget that at this stage all you have is a list, and a list is not an argument.

### TURNING A LIST OF POINTS INTO AN ARGUMENT

To turn this list into an argument what you need to do is to spice it up with some attitude. You need an angle. You need, in other words, to develop a point of view or an opinion on this list. Again, take your cue here from the terms of the question. In this case, our main point of reference is 'love'. As a sophisticated person-about-town, you probably have many interesting opinions on the subject: use one of them. Love, you might insist, is a test of character, in which case you might argue this by proposing that all the main couplings in the play go through a period of trial until the worth of the love involved has passed the test of endurance, ending in the triple marriage in Act 5. If you are of a more cynical disposition, you might argue that all the declarations of love in the play are false – the stately love of Theseus and Hippolyta is an act of violent conquest, the courtly love of Demetrius and Helena ends in matrimony only because Demetrius remains drugged up to his eyeballs, the fatherly love of Egeus for Hermia only persists because he is prevented from killing or exiling her under the orders of Theseus, and so on.

Whatever angle you choose, the important point is that you actually propose an argument and that you can support it. Thus, in the case of this question – 'Discuss the different types of love in *A Midsummer Night's Dream*' – you could just state that there are five types of love in the play – stately, courtly, supernatural, tragic and fatherly – and give examples of each. This would be a reasonable response, but a good one would involve you suggesting an overall proposal about these different types, such as that at bottom (no pun intended) they are all in some way deceitful or false.

**To turn a list of points into an argument, develop a point of view or opinion on that list.**

## THREE OPINIONS WHICH DO NOT COUNT AS GOOD ARGUMENTS

Arguments, then, are a way of connecting otherwise unrelated points together in the form of an opinion. There are, however, three types of opinion which do not usually count as reasonable arguments:

1   Arguments that merely repeat or describe the plot.
2   Arguments about how much you like or dislike the text.
3   Arguments which bear no relation to the text.

**1**   Arguments which merely repeat or describe the story of the text you are writing about are not really arguments at all. They are actually a form of paraphrase. Except with certain forms of poetry, the story is generally obvious for anyone who has read it, and believe me, your teacher will no doubt have read it many times already. Thus, for example, if we state that 'James Joyce's "Araby" is a story about a boy who visits a bazaar', we are not presenting an argument but paraphrasing the plot. If, on the other hand, we state that 'James Joyce's "Araby" is a story about the aesthetic power of religion', we are no longer merely recounting the plot but, rather, advancing a debatable proposition which the rest of your essay should be concerned to support.

**A paraphrase of the plot is not an argument.**

**2**   The second type of argument which will fail to score highly is one that centres around an expression of how much you value the text. For example, '*The Whitsun Weddings* is a thoroughly smashing collection of poems that made me weep uncontrollably' does not count as an argument. Similarly, '*The Rainbow* was such a boring book I didn't even notice when my head fell off' does not count as an argument either. Your tutors will no doubt be interested to know whether you like a text or not. However, save such declarations for your conclusion or for the classroom.

Even when your argument is slightly more subtle than the above examples, you must be careful to avoid evaluating the text as part of the focus of your thesis. So, for example, take the argument that

**Stating whether you like or dislike a text is not an argument.**

'Caryl Churchill's two-act structure in *Top Girls* fails to highlight the historical oppression of women'. The word 'fail' here is an explicit evaluation of the play. Rather than make a value judgement about the text, you might simply state as your argument that 'Caryl Churchill's two-act structure in *Top Girls* is designed to highlight the historical oppression of women'. The bulk of your essay will prove this thesis and in your conclusion, if you feel strongly about it, you can explain either why you think it fails to do what it should, or why you think it is terrific. In the main, though, you may assume that when your teachers ask you to study a particular text they are also implicitly affirming the worth of that text. Its value is therefore decided in advance and no longer a matter for argument. So feel free to voice your opinion, but don't make it the mainstay of your essay.

**3** The third type of argument which registers rather poorly with tutors is one that fails either to make any sense at all or bears no clear relation to the text you are writing about. Thus, for example, the proposal that '*Macbeth* is about the suffering

**A proposal for which you have no proof is not an argument.**

of two homeless bananas during the Cold War' seems to bear no relation to the concerns of the Shakespearean play we all know and love.

Whilst this is somewhat of an extreme example, it does highlight the difficulty of knowing what counts as a meritorious argument and what does not. The simple answer to this centres around the question of proof: if you have evidence to support your argument then it counts as a good one. Thus, if we take the above proposal about *Macbeth* we can quickly discount it because there are no bananas in the play, not even symbolic ones, and it was written some four centuries or so before the outbreak of the Cold War.

## SO YOU THINK YOU KNOW A GOOD ARGUMENT FROM A BAD ONE

Well, look at the following examples and decide which you think are good and which bad – and explain why.

1   Brian Friel's *Translations* examines the importance of a nation's language to a nation's politics.
2   Shakespeare's *The Tempest* is about the rights and wrongs of colonialism.
3   Dickens's *Hard Times* is a great comic novel but a poor social critique.
4   Wordsworth's *The Prelude* is a lengthy meditation about the author.
5   Erich Maria Remarque's *All Quiet on the Western Front* is about World War I.
6   Blake's *Songs of Innocence* and *Songs of Experience* juxtapose the two contrary states of the human soul.

Taking them in order, see if you agree with my evaluations of these arguments.

**1**    This is a good argument because it proposes a debatable thesis concerning the themes of Friel's play. However, a really good argument would root the argument about the play's themes in a discussion of the play's techniques. In this case, it could be argued that Friel employs the device of the outsider (Owen, who is a stranger both at home and abroad) in order to make his point. The thesis could be reworded to make mention of this, for example, 'Brian Friel's *Translations* uses the conceit of the outsider in order to examine the importance of a nation's language to its politics'.

**2**    This argument is more good than bad, but it does hedge its bets somewhat in its refusal to confirm or deny the bias of the play's treatment of colonialism. This makes it sound rather vague as a thesis, a problem compounded by the use of the phrase 'is about'. A more productive approach to take in cases such as these is to argue that the text takes an *active* role in rehearsing whatever dilemma or ambiguity is at issue. Ask yourself what the text *does* with its themes. In this instance, then, you might rephrase the argument to state that 'Shakespeare's *The Tempest* dramatizes the conflict between the colonized and the colonizer'.

> **Don't just say a text 'is about' certain themes – state what it does to these themes.**

**3**    However much you might agree with this argument, it is not a good one for the purposes of essay writing because it proposes two value judgements – 'great' and 'poor'. On the other hand, the argument does advance a useful antithesis between *Hard Times* as a comedy and *Hard Times* as a social critique. With this in mind, the argument might be rephrased to contend that 'Dickens's *Hard Times* is a social critique written in the form of a comedy'.

**4**    This is a very poor argument. To begin with, the adjective 'lengthy' here betrays a negative value judgement about Wordsworth's poem, indicating that it is too long. It is also worth noting that the length of a poem does not constitute a substantial basis for an argument. Furthermore, the phrase 'meditation on himself' is a weak description of what is technically more of an autobiographical poem. As the autobiographical form of the poem is obvious to anyone who has read it, this argument ultimately seems less like a debatable proposition than a statement of fact. A more promising approach would be to form a view on the manner in which Wordsworth uses autobiography. In this way, you might reword the argument to propose that 'Wordsworth employs his own autobiography as a focus for exploring the different phases of life generally'.

**5**    This is another poor argument. Erich Maria Remarque's *All Quiet on the Western Front* is *set* in World War I, but it's

> **Try to use the correct technical terms when describing a text.**

not really *about* World War I. Rather it is about the experience of a small group of soldiers, and one in particular, during World War I. Again though, this amounts to no more than a paraphrase of the plot. It would be far better to combine a comment on the technique of the novel with a translation of its plot into themes. So, for example, you might say that 'Erich Maria Remarque's *All Quiet on the Western Front* utilizes the experience of an individual soldier to examine the terrible effects of trench warfare'.

**6** At first sight this seems like a fairly good argument. It offers a thesis about the themes of Blake's poems and it grounds that thesis in a discussion of their technique by mentioning the juxtaposition of the *Songs of Innocence* and *Experience* in the one volume. However, there is more to the argument than meets the eye, as those of you who have read the poems might have noticed. This is because the phrase 'the two contrary states of the human soul' is taken directly from the subtitle of Blake's book. While this is not quite cheating, it does not represent the efforts of an original thinker and it would be marked accordingly. It is far better for your grade if you think up your own argument. However, that is not to say that you can't use an author's own words as part of your argument, just as long as you make it clear that you are doing so. In this case, you might contend that 'For Blake, *Songs of Innocence* and *Songs of Experience* juxtapose "the two contrary states of the human soul", whereas what they both really represent is the triumph of experience over innocence'.

> **If your argument is taken from another source, make sure you acknowledge that source.**

If your assessments matched mine, you're well on your way to understanding what counts as a good argument and what does not. There are, however, more detailed criteria by which you can appraise the value of an argument. These can be broadly divided between three different categories, categories against which your tutors will implicitly assess the worth of an argument. They include an argument's *coherency*, its *connectivity* and its *complexity*. These are the three Cs and they are the subject of the next three chapters.

**Always ask yourself:**
- ✔ Is my argument a debatable proposition or thesis, rather than merely a statement of fact?
- ✔ Is my argument about the themes of the text, the techniques used to portray those themes, or both?
- ✔ Is my argument a paraphrase of the plot, an expression of like or dislike for the text, or one which cannot be proved by evidence from the text?

*Of the three Cs – coherency, connectivity and complexity – coherency is undoubtedly the most important for creating a good argument. The coherency of an argument refers to its logic and consistency. A coherent argument is either an argument that does not contradict itself or an argument that is not contradicted by the evidence. If an argument is incoherent it will be unpersuasive to your teacher and will receive a poor mark.*

## THE VALUE OF A COHERENT ARGUMENT

If you recall the analogy between a courtroom and an essay, you can immediately see the value of a coherent argument. Suppose you were defending a client on a charge of murder. You had spent weeks proving that your client was nowhere near the scene of the crime at the time of the murder, and then you suddenly produced an eye-witness who saw your client with a knife in his hands, dripping with blood, screaming, 'I did it, I did it!' Your whole case would collapse, and it would do so because you were being incoherent, because you were arguing that your client was innocent while proving his guilt. Similarly, in literary criticism you must maintain a coherent argument in order to help persuade your teacher of the validity of that argument.

> **If your argument is incoherent, it will also be unpersuasive.**

## KEEPING AN ARGUMENT COHERENT IN THE FACE OF THE EVIDENCE

The most common reason why arguments become incoherent is that they are undermined by a piece of evidence that seems to prove the opposing case. Returning to our earlier example, 'Discuss the different types of love in *A Midsummer Night's Dream*', let us suppose that you have decided to argue that all the love in the play is ultimately false. Having decided on this as your argument, do not then contradict yourself by asserting that the courtly love of Lysander and Hermia is the exception to that rule. Instead, you have three choices:

**1   Abandon the argument.** You can abandon the argument because, after all, if a major piece of evidence contradicts your opinion then it may well be an unsound one. You should only need to abandon an argument at the planning stage because by the time you begin to write your essay you should have ironed out all the contradictions. Indeed, part of planning an essay involves testing an argument against the evidence in order to see whether or not it is valid. In the case of this essay, your first hypothesis might be that *A Midsummer Night's Dream* dramatizes the triumph of love over adversity. However, when you compare this against the evidence you find that, for example, the coupling of Hippolyta and Theseus is based on his violent conquest of her rather than mutually shared sentiment. You change your argument to accommodate the new evidence, perhaps settling for the thesis that all the love in the play is false.

> **If a major piece of evidence contradicts your argument then you need to abandon the argument and start over again.**

**2   Ignore the evidence.** You can ignore the evidence, a tactic not uncommon in even the most erudite literary criticism, if only because it is impossible to account for everything in a single essay. You will never be able to produce an argument that is completely water-tight. Fifty years ago some of the most respected critics in the world sought with each analysis to incorporate all the inconsistencies and paradoxes of a text within a unifying argument. Today, some of the most respected critics in the world have shown how the unity of these arguments is wholly false. So do not think you need to saturate a text with your argument, accounting for all of its different features, because it cannot be done. Nevertheless, having said this, if you have to ignore a major feature of the text in order to use a particular argument then that argument is patently flawed and you should abandon it.

**3   Interpret the evidence in a different way.** You can try to accommodate the evidence to your point of view. This is where your powers of persuasion will really be put to the test because you must argue that what looks like an exception to the rule of your argument is really a piece of evidence which supports that argument. You can do this because the interpretation of language is not bound by objective rules. For example, what is the stronger form of anger – 'fury', 'rage' or 'wrath'? As there is no right or wrong answer to this, you could argue the case for any of them and the effectiveness of your argument would depend on how persuasive you were. In this instance, where the courtly love of Lysander and Hermia might be interpreted as an exception to your argument that all the love in the play is false, you need to convince the reader of your essay that it is also a delusive and dishonest coupling. You might therefore assert that not only is courtly love a theatricalized and therefore insincere form of love, but that Lysander proves this with his infidelity half way through the play. If that is not convincing enough on its own, then part of its persuasiveness comes from the fact that you make this point within the context of an argument about the rest of the play for which you have ample evidence.

Whatever you decide to do when faced with conflicting evidence, your primary responsibility is to maintain a coherent argument by adducing only that evidence which supports it.

### KEEPING AN ARGUMENT COHERENT IN THE FACE OF OPPOSING ARGUMENTS

It is generally not a good idea to start your essay by stating one argument and to finish it by proposing another opposing one – in the same way that it's just not very convincing if a lawyer in court is both counsel for the defence and counsel for the prosecution. There is, however, one form of exception to this rule. That is when a really outstanding essay takes into account arguments that contradict the one it is upholding. But it does so only to prove how limited, false or otherwise inconsequential all other arguments are.

> **An outstanding essay will take into account opposing arguments, but only to prove them inferior to the argument it ultimately advances.**

It is similar to the way in a courtroom a lawyer will attend most politely to a witness for the opposing counsel by bolstering the witness's ego, soothing his or her nerves and generally treating that witness as if what she or he says is really genuine and important. However, having lulled him or her into a false sense of security, the lawyer then forces the witness to reveal something which turns out to contradict what she or he had been saying ten minutes earlier.

If this ploy is satisfying and enjoyable to watch on film, it is equally effective when used as a technique in essay writing. In our *A Midsummer Night's Dream* essay, for example, you could accomplish something like this by highlighting the many ways in which the play *seems* to celebrate the sanctity of love, such as alluding to the triple marriage celebration with which it concludes, before you then show in compelling detail how this celebration is actually a cruel and cynical sham.

To see how effective this technique can be, take a look at the following extracts from the conclusions of two essays answering another type of question about love: 'Discuss the ways in which love ultimately triumphs in Ian McEwan's *Enduring Love*'.

 **A)** Love certainly does triumph at the end of Ian McEwan's *Enduring Love*. The most obvious way it does this is in the relationship between Joe and Clarissa. They split up during the course of the novel because of a series of misunderstandings and because of Jed. When Jed is locked up so is his hate, and Joe and Clarissa's love for each other triumphs and they get back together. Also, their love for children, which had been thwarted because they could not conceive, is finally realized at the end when they adopt a child. As the title suggests, it is an enduring or long-lasting love which puts up with a lot but ultimately remains.

 **B)** It is certainly possible to make a case that love ultimately triumphs in *Enduring Love* – Joe and Clarissa are reconciled, their love of children is satisfied by adoption and even Jean Logan finally learns that her husband actually did love her. However, as the ambiguity of the title hints, love may last – it endures – but at the price of becoming suffering and thus not really love at all, but rather something to be endured. The triumph of love in this last sense belongs to the senseless passion which Jed has for Joe which results in Jed being institutionalized. He has the last or ultimate word in the novel in the second Appendix. The rather more muted triumph of the love between Joe and Clarissa is nothing more than an aside in the first Appendix whose scientific tone is in tune with rational kind of love those two end up with. Finally, Jean Logan finds that her husband's love for her endured or triumphed over her doubts about his fidelity, but that it is a hollow triumph because he is no longer there to forgive her. In this sense love triumphs, but it is a victory at great cost.

Can you see the difference between these two essays? Essay A advances a fairly straightforward argument which proposes that love does ultimately triumph in McEwan's novel. This argument is backed up with evidence from the text and is summarized quite neatly. Essay B also advances the same argument, which is basically an assertion of the assumption in the question, and it does so using much of the same evidence.

However, Essay B then goes on to challenge the question's assumption, utilizing the ambiguity of the title as a departure point. The 'triumph of love' is shown to be a disaster and the meaning of 'ultimately' becomes as questionable as where the end of McEwan's novel actually lies. In other words, having set up and proved the argument contained in the question, Essay B then rebuts it point for point, amalgamating that argument within a larger, opposing thesis. By doing this, Essay B opens up *Enduring Love* to a far more complex analysis and is able to advance a more sophisticated argument than Essay A.

> **Taking into account an opposing argument does not leave your thesis incoherent if you rebut the opposing argument point by point.**

Indeed, there are several advantages to the technique of taking into account an argument opposing your own:

1  It demonstrates your ability to consider the same issue from different perspectives.
2  It adds depth to your essay by providing dramatic contrast.
3  It illustrates your competence to resolve contradictory view-points.
4  It stops you from steam-rolling over a text with a single argument and instead keeps you alert to the ambiguities of a novel, poem or play.
5  It gives your teacher two arguments for the price of one.

Using this technique (if appropriate) will result in a far better essay and a far better grade.

**Always ask yourself:**
✔  Is my argument contradicted by any evidence in the text?
✔  Is my argument contradicting itself?
✔  Is my argument more persuasive than the counter-argument?

## 4

# Making a connected argument

*The second criterion against which the value of an argument will be judged is its connectivity. The connectivity of an argument refers to its ability to account for different features of a text. The greater the connectivity of an argument, the more features it will be able to explain and link together in an overall pattern, the more persuasive your argument will be.*

## THE PRINCIPLE OF CONNECTIVITY

Back in the courtroom (where you seem to spend an awful lot of your time these days), you can see how a highly connected argument is also a forceful argument. If you are prosecuting a woman for murder and you have forensic evidence that proves she held the gun that killed the victim, you have a reasonable case. If you are also able to prove she was at the murder scene when the crime was committed, your case seems even more convincing. But you don't stop there, because you are a merciless lawyer.

You also produce a motive, a reason why she might reasonably have wanted to kill the victim. Furthermore, you have eye-witnesses to a quarrel between the victim and the defendant. You have expert testimony that proves the defendant is a homicidal maniac. You have closed-circuit television pictures that show her committing the crime. The connectivity rating for your argument that she is guilty is going off the scale. You have connected the defendant to the murder in so many ways that your argument is more compelling than a force-ten gale. The defendant breaks down in the dock and confesses, 'I'm guilty, I admit it, just stop!' The case is won, you are famous and riches are yours for evermore.

In the slightly less lucrative world of literary criticism, the same principle of connectivity applies. Let me show you what I mean. Imagine you have decided to argue that in Shakespeare's *Richard II* language *is* action. To begin with you might state the fairly obvious point that actions, such as the battle scenes, are conveyed through language rather than through an actual action on stage. You then might add that the plot progresses through what characters *say* rather than what they *do*. For example, in the case of the disintegration of Richard's identity, we hear him give up the crown before we see him do it, making language take precedence over action.

So far, so good. But you don't stop there, because you are a merciless literary analyst. You go on to point out that political conflict in the play is given verbal expression, so that rather than showing pistols drawn at dawn, conflict is dramatized in terms of images, such as tending a garden. Next you argue that characters move, geographically speaking, by saying that they do, such as when Richard makes the

> **The more features of a text you are able to connect together with your argument, the more persuasive it will be.**

return trip to Ireland. You even point out that a sense of place is evoked through its description, rather than through props. Each point you make, then, includes more and more of the play, and each time you are able to make reference to more of the play, your argument about the play becomes more convincing because it is able to connect more of the play's features together.

The obverse is also true. Suppose you are the leading light of your class, known for your daring interpretations of texts and, carried away with your own sense of infamy, you decide to argue that James Joyce's 'Araby' is really a story about ten jellyfish who go on a package holiday to Peru. This is admirable stuff, no doubt, but for all your ingenuity you are unable to make the case stick. The reason for this is that your thesis

> **If your argument can only account for a few of a text's features, it will be unpersuasive.**

cannot account for any of the features of the text: it contains no jellyfish, no package holidays, no Peru. Your argument lacks, in other words, any connectivity.

### HOW DO YOU ESTABLISH A STRONG SENSE OF CONNECTIVITY?

The simple answer is that you forge connections between the different parts of the text, and the way you do this is by employing *concepts*. A concept is an idea or a category of thought which enables you to link otherwise unrelated points together, just as a surname is a way of connecting otherwise completely different people in a family. For example, 'fruit' is the concept that links 'apples' and 'oranges'. 'Food' is

> **Use concepts to link unrelated parts of a text together.**

the concept that links together 'fruit' and 'meat'. 'Basic necessities' is the concept that links together 'food' and 'shelter', and so on.

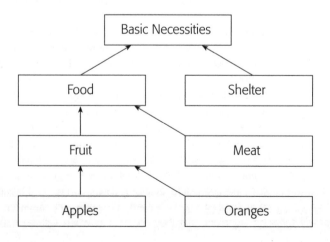

As you can see from these examples, a concept is a form of paraphrase. For example, the concept of 'apples' is shorthand for *all apples* regardless of whether they are Granny Smiths or Golden Delicious, big or small, sweet or sour. Similarly, 'fruit' is a paraphrase for all fruit, including here the concepts of 'apples' and 'oranges'. It is like your surname, which is a paraphrase or shorthand for your whole family, whether or not you are like your mum or dad, sister or brother.

When you are writing an essay, you are basically rewriting the text in paraphrase or shorthand. But instead of paraphrasing the plot, you are paraphrasing the themes of the novel, poem or play in terms of a concept. If you are writing about Caryl Churchill's *Top Girls*, for example, your argument might be that it is about the oppression of women. Now there are many different types of oppression in *Top Girls*, ranging from physical to mental. But your concept – 'the oppression of women' – accounts for them all. It is a summary, paraphrase or shorthand way of connecting all these different forms of oppression in the play together. This is what every argument should do.

> **An argument is a basically a paraphrase of the text in terms of a concept.**

## SOME CONCEPTS ARE BIGGER THAN OTHERS

As you can also see in the diagram on p. 24, certain concepts are bigger than others. 'Food' is a bigger concept than 'fruit' because not only does it combine 'apples' and 'oranges' together, as fruit does, but it also connects 'apples' and 'oranges' with 'meat' in a way which the concept of 'fruit' is unable to do. Broadly speaking, then, the bigger the concept, the greater the connectivity, the more useful it is for writing an essay, the better your argument will be, the higher the grade you will receive for it.

> **The bigger the concept you use, the more parts of a text you will be able to link together.**

Let me show you what I mean. Suppose you are still writing the essay on Joyce's 'Araby' and you have abandoned the argument about jellyfish and are searching for something more substantial instead. Scrutinizing the story carefully, you notice that it makes various references to chalices and church services and cherubs and so on. What concept links all these references together? One concept that does is 'religion'. From that point you are then able to formulate the argument that 'James Joyce's "Araby" is about religion'.

OK, that's not a bad start. Your argument displays a moderate level of connectivity, insofar as it connects many of the features of the text together. However, it does not account for all of the story's features, features such as the adolescent boy's infatuation with the older girl, their anticipated meeting at the bazaar and the disappointing spectacle of the bazaar itself. What concept links these details together? One concept that does is 'promise'. All these features of the story revolve around the boy's expectations of forthcoming happiness and their failure to be fulfilled. So, from there you can formulate the argument that 'James Joyce's "Araby" is a story about promise'.

Which is all very well, but you have already decided that 'Araby' is a story about religion. Which, then, is the better argument? Quite simply, the better argument is the one that joins them both together. Let us say, for the sake of simplicity, that each of your arguments accounts for 50 per cent of the story's features respectively. What you want is an argument that accounts for 100 per cent of the story's features. All you need to do, therefore, is find a concept that connects 'religion' with 'promise'. One that fits the bill is 'faith'. 'Faith' signifies a belief in something not altogether tangible. It thus accounts nicely for both the religious aspects of the story and those concerned with the boy's infatuation.

**If you have to choose which argument to use, always go for the one that accounts for more of the text.**

Having done this, you need to form some sort of opinion on the character of 'faith' in the story. You could thus propose, for example, that ' "Araby" is about the motivational power of faith', or that ' "Araby" is about the triumph of faith over experience'. Your argument will be extremely persuasive because the concept you have chosen as the focal point of your proposal – the concept of 'faith' – is broad enough to be able to account for, and connect, all of the features of the story.

### WHAT IF I CAN'T THINK OF A CONCEPT TO LINK EVERYTHING TOGETHER?

Of course, sometimes you just won't be able to call to mind a concept that links together two other concepts as readily as you might wish. If this is the case, one particularly useful aid is a thesaurus. Simply look up the two different concepts – for example, 'religion' and 'promise' – and compare the lists of synonyms to see if they have any equivalent terms in common – such as 'faith'. You can even use a dictionary in this way, although its definitions will not be as extensive, and therefore as useful, as those of a thesaurus.

**If you can't think of a concept to link two smaller concepts together, look at the synonyms for each term in a thesaurus.**

Just to check that you've got the hang of linking different concepts together using larger concepts, try out these examples:

1   In Ian McEwan's *Enduring Love*, two of the main themes are <u>disaster</u> and <u>love</u>. What links them together?
2   In Tennessee Williams's *A Streetcar Named Desire*, three of the main themes are <u>race</u>, <u>gender</u> and <u>sexuality</u>. What links them together?
3   In Philip Larkin's *The Whitsun Weddings*, four of the main themes are <u>memory</u>, <u>regret</u>, <u>ageing</u> and <u>change</u>. What links them together?

**1**   Even though there are only two themes here, I think this is quite a difficult one. One concept that links <u>disaster</u> and <u>love</u> together is <u>intensity</u>. A disaster is an intense experience and love is an intense emotion (in fact it is sometimes spoken of as an affliction!). You could therefore argue that *Enduring Love* explores the effects of intensity on the novel's protagonists.

**2**   This example is perhaps slightly easier. You could argue that what links together <u>race</u>, <u>gender</u> and <u>sexuality</u> is <u>prejudice</u>, as all three are subject to intolerance in the play. However, a broader concept, which encompasses not only prejudice but also some of the more individual problems in the play, is <u>identity</u>. You could therefore propose that issues of identity constitute the main theme of *A Streetcar Named Desire*.

**3**   Even though there are four different concepts here – <u>memory</u>, <u>regret</u>, <u>ageing</u> and <u>change</u> – it is pretty clear that what links them all is the passing of time. You could therefore contend that the poems in *The Whitsun Weddings* are all in some way studies on the effects of the passage of time.

## MOST OF THE TEXTS YOU STUDY ALREADY HAVE A HIGH DEGREE OF CONNECTIVITY

It is also worth bearing in mind that most of the novels, plays and poems that you will be taught have been chosen precisely because they allow readers to join up their various different features using large concepts. They display what is variously termed an integrity, a wholeness or a unity of purpose, which is saying no more than that they have a high degree of connectivity.

During the last half century or so, however, many authors have abandoned the idea of connectivity, preferring instead to write books that are supposed to be more faithful to the chaos of real life. This is all very well if you are merely reading them, but if you have to write about them it makes your life a lot harder. It is worth remembering this if you are offered a choice between writing an essay on, say, Irvine Welsh's *Trainspotting* or one on James Joyce's 'Araby'. You may well love Welsh's novel and think that Joyce's short story is sentimental nonsense, but you will find it a lot easier to make the kind of conceptual connections necessary to get a good grade if you write about the latter than if you write about the former.

> **It is easier to write a good essay about a text that already displays a high degree of connectivity.**

## WHAT TO DO IF A TEXT DOES NOT ALLOW YOU TO UNITE IT USING A SINGLE CONCEPT

One more word about connectivity before I move on. There are some texts, particularly, as I say, ones written over the last fifty years or so, which take the abandonment of connectivity as their central premise. Novels by Thomas Pynchon, or short stories by Walter Abish, for example, make a point of using concepts that cannot be unified by a single concept.

If you have to write about a text like this – which you will probably only have to do at a fairly advanced level – then don't worry about finding a single, binding concept to account for all of the text's features. Instead, what you do, as they say in maths, is 'show your working out'. You simply argue that the text is deliberately contradictory and show how the different features of the novel, play or poem resist assimilation to a single concept. The chances are, however, that you will not be taught such texts for the most part, and that if you are, your teacher will alert you to their difference (probably by calling them either 'postmodernist' or 'deconstruction-ist').

**Always ask yourself:**

✔ Does my argument connect as many of the features of text together as possible?

✔ What is the most appropriate concept to describe the text?

✔ Could I use a bigger concept to link together more features of the text?

# Making a complex argument

## 5

*The third criterion against which your teachers will assess the value of an argument is its complexity. The complexity of an argument refers to its sophistication. On the one hand, this value is merely the sum of an argument's coherency and connectivity. On the other hand, it concerns the originality of an argument.*

### HOW IS COMPLEXITY THE SUM OF THE ARGUMENT'S COHERENCY AND CONNECTIVITY?

If an argument refers to other points of view, as I mentioned in Chapter 3, yet does so only to prove them limited or false, it will be a more complex argument than one that merely sticks to its own point of view. Equally, if the concept you choose as the focal point of your argument can account for all the features of a story, then your argument will be more complex, and will therefore receive a better grade, than one whose central concept only accounts for 50 per cent of a story's features.

### THE VALUE OF AN ORIGINAL ESSAY

There is, however, another component to the value of complexity, and that is originality. Most essays say the same things. This is not surprising given that most students go to the same lectures, sit in the same classrooms and talk to each other about the same essay questions. You are an individual, but your learning environment is probably not, and so a form of collective wisdom tends to prevail about every text and to be repeated in essays. This is all very well in a fact-based discipline, such as mathematics, but in one such as English Literature, which prizes the skill and strengths of argumentation more highly, it tends to reduce the impact of your chosen opinion if fifty other people have chosen it too.

> **If your essay contains the same argument as everyone else's essays it will not stand out.**

Again, it is worth bearing in mind your teacher's psyche at this point. Put yourself in her or his place and imagine marking sixty essays, fifty-five of which say the same thing. Indeed, not only do they say the same thing, but they repeat the very words that the teacher used in class. Now, your teacher may very well agree with the opinion expressed in these fifty-five essays, especially if it is his or her own opinion, but none of those essays is going to stand out from the crowd, precisely because they *are* the crowd. They will not be marked down for being unoriginal – let me be clear about that – but the five essays that display some kind of originality are more likely to be marked up, if only because they stand out and demand to be noticed.

> **You will not be marked down for an unoriginal argument but you might be marked up for an original one.**

## HOW TO WRITE AN ORIGINAL ESSAY

All of this begs the question of how you produce an original argument. If you think about it, this is not something I can give you a formula for. Nevertheless, I can provide you with some indicators of the areas you might look at to improve your essay's originality. These include:

1 Knowing the context of your answer.
2 Contesting the assumptions in the question.
3 Writing about neglected texts or questions.
4 Writing about neglected aspects of a text.
5 Cultivating your prose style.

**1　Knowing the context of your answer.** To begin with, originality depends on context. Were you to find yourself in a group of students who are all firmly convinced that 'Araby' is a story about ten jellyfish going on a package holiday to Peru, then your argument that it is actually about the power of faith would stand out like . . . well, like ten jellyfish sporting trunks and bikinis on a Peruvian beach. The point is that you need to do some of your own thinking about a text, rather than relying solely on your teacher's notes or supplementary textbooks which everyone else will also have.

**2　Contesting the assumptions in the question.** Another way of producing an original essay is to contest the assumptions in the question. Thus, for example, if you were set the essay 'Identify the ways in which *A Midsummer Night's Dream* is a celebration of love' you could challenge the assumption that it is, in fact, a celebration of love by pointing to the many deceits which I have already mentioned. Nine times out of ten, students agree with the assumptions of a question, so you stand a good chance of being original if you disagree with them. It is worth being cautious when you do this, however, as you may be treading on some very cherished toes. Your tactic here should always be to show what features of a text allow the assumption to be made in the first place – such as the triple marriage in this case – and then show how that is a false assumption. In other words, you must demonstrate that you have considered the merits of the assumption before you can declare it to be erroneous.

> **If you contest the assumptions of the question, make sure you show that you have considered them as a possibility before declaring them to be mistaken.**

**3　Writing about neglected texts or questions.** Another way of standing out from the crowd is to choose to answer an unpopular question (assuming, that is, that you have a choice). In my experience, most students will choose to write about what they consider to be the easiest book to read (if they have a choice of texts), and failing that they will answer the question that seems the easiest (usually because its topic has already been discussed in the classroom). In my experience, these choices are misguided. This is partly for the reasons I have already explained: 'easier' books have less in them to write about, and 'easier' questions only seem so because you will be repeating opinions you have already heard. The value of a question should, rather, reside in how well it allows you to write a good essay, which here means an original one. So if everyone else is answering the question on Iain Banks, then you should answer the one on Anthony Trollope, and vice versa.

> **Before you choose to write about a book you like, make sure that it is also a good book to write about.**

**4   Writing about neglected aspects of a text.** You can also make your essay original by focusing on the feature of a text which most often gets overlooked by students – its form. In general, students feel more comfortable writing about characters, stories and themes. They tend to feel less happy writing about the structural aspects of a text or the nuts and bolts that hold it all together, like grammar. This does not mean you need to devote your whole essay to a discussion of a particular text's grammatical construction, but if you at least analyse it you will make your answer stand out. So if you were writing an essay about suspense in Henry James's *The Turn of the Screw*, for example, you might spend a paragraph analysing the way in which the narrator builds dense and complex sentences using compound predicates made of several predicates at a time (and if you are not sure what a predicate is, turn to Chapter 11). The effect of this is to delay the final meaning of each sentence. In this way, you might argue, the reader is left in suspense every time she or he reads a sentence as well as while reading the novel as a whole.

> **You will make your essay stand out if you write about aspects of a text, such as its structure or grammar, which most essays ignore.**

**5   Cultivating your prose style.** Another way of improving your essay is by cultivating the style in which you write it. The best critics not only write about interesting ideas, they also produce prose which is enjoyable to read. Now, clearly your ideas are the most important feature of your essay, but if you can render those ideas in a clear and pleasurable prose style you will make them more appealing. To achieve this perhaps entails looking at an essay in entirely different way from the one you are used to – that is, instead of looking at it as a chore to be completed, look at it as an assignment to be enjoyed. No one is expecting you to start writing like F. Scott Fitzgerald or Toni Morrison, but the odd change here and there can make all the difference. Let me show you what I mean. Take a look at these opening paragraphs taken from essays answering the question 'What is the function of the rooms in Harold Pinter's *The Room* and *The Dumb Waiter*?'

> **Your essay will stand out if you take the time to write it in an enjoyable prose style.**

**A)** For Harold Pinter 'unease comes in through the door'. What does this mean for his plays *The Room* and *The Dumb Waiter*? Both dramas are set entirely in one room and, in each case, this room is seemingly the zenith of domesticity. Yet, for Rose in the former play and Gus in the latter, this homeliness is slowly consumed by a need to know who is outside the door, what they want and when they will come in. As their anxiety develops about the uncertainty of these questions it is reflected in the changing status of the rooms around them, which transform from places of safety to places of siege.

**B)** The rooms in Harold Pinter's plays *The Room* and *The Dumb Waiter* are the settings for the plays. Rose in *The Room* becomes scared as the play goes on as to what will happen. Gus in *The Dumb Waiter* also becomes scared as to what will happen as the play goes on. The fact of them being scared is shown in how the rooms change for Gus and Rose. Gus and Rose become trapped in the rooms and become scared of what is outside of them.

Which essay would you rather go on to read? I suspect it is Essay A. Both paragraphs contain roughly the same information, but Essay A is written in a more enticing prose style. Here are the differences between them:

- Essay A opens with a pithy yet relevant quotation from Harold Pinter about the topic of the question. Using a quotation like this can be an effective way to begin your essay because it provides the reader with a concrete detail which he or she can immediately get to grips with and provides you with an agenda for the rest of your introduction. It is made more effective here because it is immediately followed by a question. A question entices readers into your essay because it compels them to find out the answer. Essay B, on the other hand, begins with a rather bland statement of fact which offers no point of engagement for the reader because it is neither debatable nor intriguing.
- Essay B repeats the same words and phrases from sentence to sentence and even in the same sentence. For example, the tautologous opening sentence uses the word 'plays' twice, a word which is then repeated twice more in the following couple of sentences. Essay A, however, employs 'play' and 'drama' alternately, thus stopping the reader from becoming bored with the same word. If you can't think of a synonym yourself, use a thesaurus to find one. If you keep using proper names to describe the characters (as Essay B does with 'Gus' and 'Rose') try switching between them and personal pronouns ('he' and 'she') from time to time.
- Essay B is written using rather banal and generalized phrasing, such as 'as the play goes on' and 'the fact of them being scared'. By contrast, Essay A is composed using a variety of interesting verbs, nouns, adjectives and adverbs, for example 'zenith of domesticity' and 'slowly consumed'. This makes it more pleasurable to read. There is no need to qualify every verb with an adverb or to

make every noun an unusual one, but if you spice up your word choice here and there it will produce an impressive overall effect.
- Essay B uses no rhetorical techniques but Essay A deploys several interesting sentence constructions. For example, there is some alliteration in the fourth sentence with 'who', 'what' and 'when'. The third and fourth sentences are also made more alluring by their organization around the phrase 'seemingly . . . yet'.

All of these differences between the two essays are matters of style rather than content, but they make one a pleasurable read and the other merely a good read. It may take a little more effort to think of a distinctive word or phrase, but ultimately it will make your essay more interesting to write, more interesting to read and more likely to stand out.

### A FINAL WORD ABOUT THE COMPLEXITY OF AN ARGUMENT

Of the three criteria by which an argument will be assessed, its complexity is the least important, particularly in regard to its originality. If you can make an argument as coherent and connected as possible, then it will already be highly complex. So if you can't add some twist of originality to your argument without succumbing to the 'jellyfish trap', don't worry about it – I've given plenty of top marks to essays that didn't have a novel thought in them, and I've failed a fair few that have been nothing but startlingly new from beginning to end.

> **Having a complex argument is far less important than having a coherent and connected argument.**

### Always ask yourself:
- ✔ Is this an original argument or am I just copying what everyone else is saying?
- ✔ Have I written this argument in the most enticing way I can?
- ✔ Is this argument so original it's silly, or is it a genuinely good argument?

# Analysing a text

## 6

*If an argument forms the skeleton of your essay, then an analysis of the text puts flesh on the bones. It is the quality of your analysis that largely determines your final grade. An essay with a mediocre argument can still receive a good grade, but an essay with an outstanding argument will only get a moderate grade if its analysis of the text is mediocre. Quite simply, it is the standard of analysis which differentiates between those students who have got the hang of writing good essays and those who have not. So what exactly is 'analysis'?*

## ANALYSE, DON'T DESCRIBE

The word 'analysis' comes from the Greek word *analusis* which means 'a dissolving' or 'a loosening'. When you analyse a text you need in a sense to dissolve or loosen it. You have to break it down into its constituent parts, such as character, theme and structure, and you have to determine the relationship between these parts, showing how they work together. This is where analysis differs from description. The word 'description' comes from the Latin word *describere* which means 'to copy off' or 'to write out'. When you describe a text, you merely give an account of it, rather than explain how it works. It is the difference between saying that your car runs off an engine and showing how the expanding gases in the cylinder head drive the piston which in turn moves the connection with the crankshaft, transforming reciprocating motion into rotation, and so on.

> **When you analyse a text you need to break it down into its constituent parts and show how those parts combine to produce the effects they do.**

Understanding this distinction is vital because the most common failing of the majority of English Literature essays is their tendency to describe a text rather than analyse it. This failing can be divided into two types or tendencies – *describing the plot* and *describing the language*.

### Describing the plot

The first of these is the easiest to comprehend for it merely involves describing the plot – or, to be more accurate, paraphrasing the plot or story – of a text. As I have said in previous chapters, your teachers will have read whatever text it is you are studying many times already and they will therefore know the plot backwards. You do not get any marks for repeating, paraphrasing, summarizing or otherwise describing it. Unfortunately, many students seem to think that the first paragraph of an essay should be devoted to this task: they are wrong. I will explain this in more detail in the chapter on structuring an essay, so suffice it to say for now that your first paragraph should be concerned to outline your argument and that any description of the plot should only be for the purposes of contextualizing that argument.

> **Describing the plot is not a form of analysis.**

The only exception to this rule is, as I have also mentioned, when you are writing about a poem. The majority of the poems you will study can be thought of as overheard conversations. When you overhear a conversation, parts of it will be missing and you are unsure exactly what it is that is being discussed. So, for example, you might overhear the statement, "Bill spent six weeks recuperating but he's all right now and the whole thing worked a treat". What is lacking in this snippet of information is a context, the story behind Bill's convalescence. However, you may surmise from the information about his recuperation and 'the whole thing' working a treat that Bill had some sort of operation.

> **The analysis of poetry may sometimes require you to describe the story or context of a poem.**

Similarly, then, when you are writing about a poem you need to provide it with a context by describing the story or narrative behind it. Unlike, say, the story of Chinua Achebe's novel *Things Fall Apart*, the story behind W.B. Yeats's poem 'The Second Coming' is not obvious. Part of your job in analysing a poem is therefore to describe the story because, in the same way as you need to define the key terms of your argument, you need to make sure that your teacher shares your understanding of what the poem is about. There are some novels and short stories, such as Ernest Hemingway's 'Hills Like White Elephants', which lack a context in the same way that poems do, but, on the whole, the plots of most prose and drama writing are perfectly clear.

### Describing the language

The second type of description which mars so many essays is a little more subtle. Basically, this kind of description involves stating that a particular text, or part of it, is *something* (such as silly, simple, or sombre) without stating *why* it is, or *how* it achieves this effect. Let us say, for instance, that you argue that the opening paragraph of Edgar Allan Poe's 'The Fall of the House of Usher' sets an ominous tone for the rest of the story. This is a description of the opening paragraph. To make it an analysis you need to show how it does this.

> **In order to turn your description of the effect of a text into an analysis, you need to show how that effect is created.**

For example, you might demonstrate how most of the nouns in that opening paragraph are qualified by menacing or lugubrious adjectives. The day is 'dull, dark and soundless', the walls are 'bleak', the country is 'dreary', the tree stumps are 'ghastly', and the House of Usher itself is 'melancholy' and 'sorrowful'. You could also point out how the narrator personifies the house, granting it an uncanny stare with its 'vacant and eye-like windows'. The feelings the house produces on the narrator are also somehow eerily independent of the narrator himself. He does not feel them, rather simply *'there was* an iciness, a sinking, a sickening of the heart', an autonomous 'sense of insufferable gloom pervade[s]' his spirit. Finally, you might draw attention to the fact that the scene of the opening paragraph is set as 'the shades of evening drew on' 'in the autumn', both references to an impending ending – of the day and of the year respectively – and that 'autumn' is also known as 'the fall', an allusion to the fate of the House in the title.

There is clearly more that could be said here, but the level of detail you can afford to go into depends on the length of your essay and its relevance to your argument.

## THE PRINCIPLE OF ANALYSIS

Description becomes analysis when it explains the *hows* and *whys* of a text. Quite simply, *analysis is a demonstration of how and why specific words produce specific effects*. It is what should form the bulk of your essay because it is what forms the bulk of your grade.

This principle of analysis applies at all levels of your essay – that is, both in terms of your overall argument and in terms of individual pieces of evidence. Let us take your argument first. If we return to the courtroom you will quickly see why you need to demonstrate its validity. It is a big trial and you are defending a client on a charge of murder. You have listened to the prosecution making their case for two months, but finally they finish and it is your turn. You stand up, pace thoughtfully around the courtroom for a minute and turn to address the jury. 'Ladies and gentlemen of the jury,' you begin, 'my client *is* innocent!' You then return to your seat, put your feet on the desk and clasp your hands behind your head, beaming uncontrollably and winking at your client. It is clear you have finished making your case, but it is also clear that you have failed to convince anyone of its truth and your client is condemned to a lengthy stay in one of the country's fiercest penal institutions.

The reason for your failure here is quite clear: you did not demonstrate *why* your client is innocent; instead, you

> **Analysis is a demonstration of how and why specific words produce specific effects.**

merely described his condition. The same principle applies when you are writing an essay. If you argue that Shakespeare's *Hamlet* is a play about indecisiveness but you do not show why it is, then your teacher will not be persuaded of the validity of your argument and you will receive a poor grade. Most students, however, are aware of this and they endeavour to prove their argument by referring to specific parts of a text as evidence for their assertion.

If 'referring' sounds a little vague here, that is because many students are, in fact, a little vague about the evidence they adduce – they either describe pieces of evidence or just cite page numbers, rather than quoting from the text directly. The rule here is quite simple: if you are discussing part of a text and using it for evidence then you must quote it. Let us suppose you manage to secure another client after your last outing in court and you want to demonstrate his innocence. In order to prove this, you have enlisted the support of an expert witness who has conducted DNA tests which confirm that your client did not touch the murder weapon. Having done this, however, you do not call your expert witness to the stand, nor do you pass round copies of her report. Instead, you merely stand up and say, 'Professor Donnelly tested the weapon for my client's DNA and found it wasn't there. If you see her, you can ask her. If not, have a look at pages 5, 9 and 22 of the report she wrote some time.'

> **If you are discussing part of a text and using it for evidence then you must quote it.**

Of course, the judge will immediately rule that your evidence is inadmissible, because there is no way that your assertions about the professor's tests can be corroborated unless she is there to be interrogated independently (or a copy of her report is immediately available). Similarly, if you argue that, say, Hamlet's primary mode of address is self-referential in the play that bears his name, yet you fail to cite any instances of this, the validity of your claim is left in question.

### EVIDENCE IS NOT SELF-EXPLANATORY

However, let us suppose that you *do* quote several examples from the play in which Hamlet refers to himself, and that, furthermore, you state that these quotations show Hamlet's primary mode of address to be self-referential. This is better, but it can be better still. Evidence is not self-explanatory. Quotations, in themselves, do not show anything at all – they need to be analysed. So, in this particular case, you would need to point out the exact words and phrases which prove your point, such as 'me', 'self', 'myself' and 'I', and detail the frequency with which they occur.

> **Quotations, in themselves, do not show anything at all – they need to be analysed.**

Each point you make, then, should take the following form:

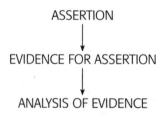

ASSERTION

↓

EVIDENCE FOR ASSERTION

↓

ANALYSIS OF EVIDENCE

Let me show you what I mean. Take a look at the following extract from an essay which tackles the question 'Examine the representation of the British Empire in Graham Greene's *The Heart of the Matter*'. See if you can follow the progression of the point as it is being made in terms of the above model.

The sense that the British Empire is in the last throes of life is underwritten throughout *The Heart of the Matter* by images of death and decay. For example, Scobie considers his own body to be 'like a grave', his room to be 'like a tomb', and the streets of the town to be 'like the arms of a skeleton', the houses as 'white as bones'. Here as elsewhere in the novel similes are used to make an explicit connection between the everyday things of Scobie's life – his body, his room, the town he lives in – and reminders of mortality and the inevitability of death, such as graves, tombs and skeletons. Scobie, of course, represents British colonialism in the novel, he is a senior official in its administration, and yet these images are all seen from his point of view. He does not see progress and the advance of civilization everywhere he looks, but seemingly endless 'vultures' as if waiting to 'pick the bones of the Empire'.

Can you see how the point is constructed?

- **Assertion** The first sentence outlines the assertion, which is that the decay of the Empire is manifest in images of death in the novel.
- **Evidence for assertion** The next sentence provides some examples of the evidence for this assertion. Any of you who have read the novel will know that there are in fact many more instances of this kind of description, but three or four examples are enough to support a point.
- **Analysis of evidence** The essay then analyses the evidence. First of all this involves detailing what kind of evidence this is – in this case, similes – and showing how similes work – by making an explicit comparison. Secondly, the essay connects the point of view of the similes with Scobie, and it connects Scobie with the point of view of the Empire. It is only at this stage that the assertion is proved, establishing in the reader's mind the link between the images of death and the impending death of British colonialism. The second clause of the last sentence is a bit of poetic speculation, but given the context of the rest of the point it does not seem inappropriate.

You should try, wherever possible, to construct all your points like this. It is the last of these three steps that is the hardest to accomplish, but the technique for doing so is relatively straightforward – keep asking questions of the text. Interrogate every paragraph, query each sentence, examine every word, scrutinize each piece of punctuation until you have your answer.

**Always ask yourself:**
✔ Am I describing the text or analysing it?
✔ Is every point backed up with evidence?
✔ Is every piece of evidence backed up with analysis?

# Structuring an essay

## 7

*You will no doubt have been told a million times that you should always plan your essays before you write them. The reason for this, so the argument goes, is that it will make your life easier if you know what you are going to write and where you are going to write it. While I would not wish to disagree with this particular piece of wisdom, I will say that it does not really matter whether you plan your essay or not, because what really counts is whether your essay looks like it has been planned or not. The whole point of a plan is not that it makes your life easier when writing your essay (although it should do); rather, the point of a plan is that it provides a structure for your essay, making it easy to read for your teacher.*

## THE OVERALL ESSAY STRUCTURE

There are basically just two parts to an essay structure – the overall structure, and the structure of each paragraph. The overall structure is made up of individual paragraphs. Perhaps the most effective way to understand this is to think of each paragraph as a point in your argument. Your argument is what forms the overall structure of your essay; it is the sum of its parts, or paragraphs. This works in the same way as lawyers make a case for or against a defendant. Each witness or piece of evidence is a paragraph in the overall structure of their argument, their argument being whether or not the defendant is guilty. Your essay, like a lawyer's case, should be composed of a series of individual but related points that form and inform an argument.

When you have conceived your argument, therefore, you need to subdivide it into its relevant points. You may, to use a common model, visualize this as a spider's

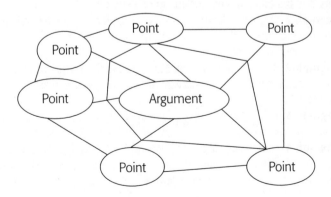

**Your argument is what forms the overall structure of your essay and each paragraph should be a point in that argument.**

web. At the centre of the web lies the main argument, sticking out of which are the different strands or points of the argument.

All the insights and evidence you have relating to a specific point should be grouped together in one paragraph. In an essay of between 1000 and 1500 words you can expect to have about five to seven paragraphs. In an essay of between 500 and 1000 words you will be more likely to write about four to six paragraphs. Your overall essay structure should then look something like this:

INTRODUCTION
PARAGRAPH 1
PARAGRAPH 2
PARAGRAPH 3
PARAGRAPH 4
PARAGRAPH 5
CONCLUSION

Don't forget to leave a line between the end of one paragraph and the beginning of the next one. Ideally, your teacher should be able to read the first sentence of each paragraph only and still be able to follow the general flow of the argument. In order to achieve this you should also try and order your paragraphs in terms of the development of your argument so that each point follows logically on from the previous one. In other words, Paragraph 2 should follow on logically from Paragraph 1, Paragraph 3 should follow on logically from Paragraph 2, and so on. Let me show you what I mean.

The following scheme shows the first sentence of each paragraph from an essay answering the question, 'Discuss the ways in which Geoffrey Chaucer's *The Wife of Bath's Prologue and Tale* is a struggle for "maistrie" '.

- **Introduction** Chaucer's *The Wife of Bath's Prologue and Tale* dramatizes the struggle between two definitions of "maistrie" – one, a form of power over others, and the other, the full command of a subject.
- **Paragraph 1** In Chaucer's time only men were permitted to read and assume mastery of the biblical, classical and political tracts which were used to enforce the subjugation of women.
- **Paragraph 2** Ironically, the Wife of Bath employs the same anti-female tracts used to dominate her as a subversive way of gaining mastery over her husbands.
- **Paragraph 3** Using her strength and sexuality, the Wife of Bath augments the rhetorical power she has over her husbands with a physical mastery.
- **Paragraph 4** Having subverted her husbands' authority, the Wife of Bath goes on to use her mastery of argumentation and storytelling in order to gain the ascendancy for her views on sexual politics amidst the rest of the pilgrims.

- **Conclusion** All of the Wife of Bath's different tactics result in a another type of mastery – a victory for her in the battle of the sexes.

Could you follow the argument from just these first sentences alone? The Introduction defines the main terms of the question and sets out the main argument. Paragraph 1 begins by detailing an aspect of this argument. Keeping the central thesis in sight, the opening sentence of Paragraph 2 offers a twist on the point made in Paragraph 1. Paragraph 3 then goes on to supplement the point of Paragraph 2, reinforcing its argument with a different type of evidence. Following on from this, Paragraph 4 widens the scope of the essay's main proposal, allowing it to include a discussion of the text's form and technique. All of this is capped by a Conclusion which neatly summarizes the various aspects of the central argument.

Try extracting the first line of each paragraph from some of your previous essays and see if you can follow your own argument from these alone. If you can't, it probably means they were not as easy to read and follow as they might have been. Of course, not every argument is susceptible to this linear or chronological approach. Nevertheless, you should still be able to extract the main points of an argument from your essay's opening sentences. If you are still not sure about this technique, look up a few articles in some of the more serious newspapers where you should find it in daily use.

## THE STRUCTURE OF PARAGRAPHS

If you think of your essay as a meal, then each paragraph is a course in that meal. It therefore needs to be easily digestible. Most of us can't eat everything on a plate at one gulp, nor do we eat the ketchup before we eat the chips before we eat the salt before we eat the vinegar, and we tend not to mix ice-cream with cabbage, and so on. Instead, we prefer bite-sized chunks of complementary foods. Each paragraph of your essays should be such a chunk.

Basically, each paragraph should focus on one main point, which should, in turn, illuminate or support your overall argument from a specific and explicit angle. This point should be backed up with evidence quoted from the text, which you should then analyse. Following this, you detail any other minor points which relate to the main point of the paragraph but which are not big enough in themselves to warrant

> **Each paragraph should focus on one main point and be supported with evidence from the text.**

a whole paragraph. As a general rule, the minimum length of each paragraph is three sentences. Each paragraph, then, should correspond in large part to the following structure:

MAIN POINT OF PARAGRAPH AND RELEVANCE TO ARGUMENT

EVIDENCE FOR POINT

ANALYSIS OF EVIDENCE

MINOR, BUT RELATED, POINTS AND EVIDENCE FOR THEM

The reason why each paragraph should be 'headlined' with reference to the overall argument is to keep that argument in the reader's mind, thereby enabling them to see the relevance of the rest of the paragraph. It is always better to be explicit and sure that your teacher can follow your reasoning, rather than leave the connection between an individual paragraph and the argument of the essay implicit and risk your teacher losing the thread.

## INTRODUCTIONS AND CONCLUSIONS

One of the biggest causes of anxiety for students writing essays is the question of what to put in the introduction and conclusion. There is, however, no need to worry because almost every introduction and conclusion will follow the same format.

### Introductions

Introductory paragraphs are just that – a way of introducing the reader to your argument. And just as you tend not to ask someone if they like their eggs sunny side up before you have even asked if they like eggs at all, you should keep the introduction general and let the body of the essay sort out the details. To this end, define the terms of the question, outline your argument and indicate how this responds to the essay topic. Clarity is essential here more than anywhere else in your essay, because if your argument is not clearly stated at this stage then your teacher will not be able to understand the relevance of the rest of your analysis. One thing you do not need to do in an introduction is describe the story. Describing the story tends to muddy the waters of your argument, either impairing its clarity or, even worse, leading you to think that you do not need to outline your argument at all because you have already filled up the available space for an introduction. The only exceptions to this golden rule are where you are specifically being asked to contextualize a passage, or where you are analysing a poem the context of which is unclear, and in both cases your description will form part of your argument.

> **Use the introduction to define the terms of the question, outline your argument and indicate how this responds to the essay topic.**

### Conclusions

The conclusion of your essay should be kept relatively brief. Its function is simply to convey the sense of an ending – like coffee and mints after a good meal. To this end, you can paraphrase or sum up your argument, perhaps indicating at this stage quite how well you think a particular text produces the effects that you say it does. Unless you have a very good conclusion – and if so, why isn't it in the body of your essay? – *keep it brief*: most conclusions outstay their welcome by repeating at needless length material already in the essay.

## HOW TO QUOTE FROM A TEXT

The rules for quoting are quite simple: *every point should have a quotation,* and *every quotation should have a point.* In other words, every time you make a point it should be supported with evidence from the text, but the evidence you quote should only be that which is relevant to the point you are making. You will therefore almost certainly need to edit your quotations. Do not worry about this – you are not violating the sacred integrity of a text, you are merely doing your job. Thus, for example, if you state that a particular passage conveys a sombre atmosphere, do not quote the whole passage, just those words which are relevant to your point, such as 'funereal', 'dark', 'grey', 'lugubrious', and so on.

> **Every point should have a quotation, and every quotation should have a point.**

If you need to quote a sentence or line from a text, but you only need to refer to the beginning and end of it, use an *ellipsis* (three dots) to indicate that you have omitted certain words. So, for example, if the sentence you were quoting from was, 'The shops were closing fast, and lights began to shine from the upper windows, as the neighbours went to bed', you might quote it as, 'The shops were closing fast... as the neighbours went to bed'.

Of course, don't forget to use quotation marks to indicate that you are in fact quoting from a text.

- Quotations should go in *single* quotation marks, e.g. 'Gatsby looked at the green light'.
- Single quotation marks should be used for quotations within your own prose and double quotation marks should be used for quotations within a quotation, e.g. 'Gatsby said, "I want to repeat the past" '.
- Indent lengthy quotations, roughly anything over three lines long. To indent a quotation, leave a bigger margin than for the main body of your essay and a line of space before and after the quotation.
- Do not use quotation marks for an indented quotation, but apply the rule in the second point above for quotations or speech occurring within the extract.
- Quote poetry (or dramatic verse, such as Shakespeare) as if it were verse, and not prose. To this end, use a slash to indicate the end of a line if it is not a lengthy quotation, e.g. 'Had we but world enough, and time,/ This coyness, Lady, were no crime'.
- Provide page references in brackets after every quotation from a novel or short story. Provide act, scene and line numbers in brackets for every quotation from a play or long poem where possible, and if they do not exist, use page numbers instead.
- Remember that 'quote' is a verb, and that 'quotation' is the noun.

**Always ask yourself:**
- ✔ Does the introduction clearly state my argument and define the terms of the question?
- ✔ Is my essay structured so that the argument is easy to follow?
- ✔ Is every point backed up with a pertinent quotation and is each quotation strictly relevant?

# SECTION 2

# Technical language

## 8

# Analysing language

*Many questions ask that you examine, discuss, analyse or otherwise look at the language of a text or a specific passage. This is obviously a bit of a catch-all question as you cannot very well scrutinize the spaces in between the words to look for meaning. Furthermore, you are implicitly expected to analyse the language of a text whatever the question says explicitly. So, to what does 'analysing language' specifically refer?*

## DICTION

Well, it refers to a variety of a text's features, beginning with *diction*. 'Diction' is often used as a synonym for 'elocution', but its primary meaning designates the choice and use of words in writing or speech. As the hefty size of your average thesaurus suggests, the English language is rich with words that can be substituted for each other. This means that when we write, we are continually making subtle choices about which words we use and, in so doing, we are, consciously or unconsciously, refining the meaning of the message we are trying to create. When you are writing an essay, therefore, you need to state what effect the use of a particular word, or group of words, has.

> **Diction refers to the choice of words or type of vocabulary used in a poem, play or novel.**

For example, if you were writing an essay on Henrik Ibsen's *A Doll's House*, you would probably want to attend to the 'pet' names with which Thorvald demeans Nora. These names include 'skylark', 'squirrel' and 'squanderbird'. Remembering that it is not enough merely to state that these extracts show how poorly Thorvald thinks of Nora, you must now demonstrate why they do. This is not always an easy task, but if you are stuck, try asking yourself: what difference does it make using one particular word rather than another, similar one?

In this case, therefore, we might ask what other animal names Thorvald could call Nora. Suppose we substitute 'lion', 'eagle' and 'scorpion' for 'skylark', 'squirrel' and 'squanderbird'. These names would suggest that Thorvald saw Nora very

> **Ask yourself what difference it makes using one particular word rather than another, similar one.**

differently from how the pet names he actually uses suggest he sees her. In other words, Thorvald's diction, his choice of words, reveals a specific attitude towards Nora.

## CONNOTATIONS AND DENOTATIONS

However, we are not finished yet. We have still not identified exactly what it is about the word 'skylark' which is demeaning in a way that the word 'lion', albeit still an animal type, is not. The difference here – as everywhere else – depends upon the division between a word's *denotation* and its *connotation*. A word's denotation is what the word refers to; a word's connotation is what is implied or associated with that word.

> **A word's denotation is what the word refers to; a word's connotation is what is implied or associated with that word.**

Here, then, we might say that while 'lion' *denotes* a large, savannah-dwelling cat, it *connotes* power, majesty, ferocity, and so on. Likewise, whereas 'skylark' *denotes* a song bird, it *connotes* (especially in comparison to 'lion') fragility, flightiness, whimsicality, and so on. Indeed, we can see that what unites the animal names by which Thorvald refers to Nora are their connotations of tininess and lightness and it is this that makes them demeaning.

It is almost always the case that you can identify the purpose of a text's diction – that is, the effect of the specific words it employs – by attending not just to the denotative properties of the words, but also, more importantly, to their connotations. Should you be unable to think of any connotations for a given word, consult your thesaurus and trace the implicit connections of each synonym.

## PATTERNS

Another key aspect of language to which you must attend while analysing a text are the *patterns* it makes. A text's patterning refers to the connections forged by both the simple repetition of a word and the conceptual interplay between related words. Taking repetition first, it may be boldly stated that the more often a word is repeated (usually excluding articles, prepositions and so forth), the more significant it is to the overall meaning of the text you are studying. Thus, for example, the word 'fool' is mentioned 47 times in *King Lear*, 'secret' occurs over 50 times in Joseph Conrad's *The Secret Agent*, and the phrase 'So it goes' is repeated over 100 times in Kurt Vonnegut's *Slaughterhouse-Five*.

> **The pattern of a text is formed either by the simple repetition of a word or by the interplay between related words.**

In what ways a repeated word or phrase is significant depends upon its context. If it is repeated by a character, it may afford you an insight only to that particular character, rather than the whole text. Uriah Heep in Charles Dickens's *David Copperfield*, for example, confesses to being 'humble' in almost every sentence to the point where you rightly suspect he is trying to persuade others of a feeling that is not entirely sincere. Returning to *A Doll's House*, Thorvald's constant use of 'little', both as part of an appellation and as a way to describe Nora's activities, forms part of a larger pattern in the play by which her concerns are trivialized and the injustice of patriarchy is illustrated.

Patterns are also formed by the conceptual interplay between related words. Such patterns are not as difficult to understand as they sound, for, as we have already seen, no word exists in isolation. It is the connections between words, in terms of their denotations and connotations, which form the greater part of all patterns in English Literature.

If we return to *A Doll's House*, we can see that Thorvald continually refers to Nora using the metaphor of possession. She is 'my most treasured possession', he avows, 'this wonderful beauty that's mine, all mine'. At one point he even exclaims, 'take a good look at her, she's worth looking at'. He treats her, in other words, as if she were an ornamental object in his possession. It is a status she admits to having accepted when she declares that she was 'a doll-child' and then 'a doll-wife'. This metaphorical position is then reinforced in the play by the physical possession Thorvald takes over Nora, such as locking the door on her, denying her the keys to the mailbox, and abruptly escorting her from the dance. All of these features of the play contribute to, and derive from, the central concept that *A Doll's House* is concerned to interrogate – the dependent and subordinate status of women in nineteenth-century Norway. There is a barely a word, stage direction or prop in the whole play that does not assist in developing this pattern.

## REGISTER

Having looked at the diction and patterns of a text, you should also analyse the *register* in which a particular text is written. The register of a text simply refers to the type of language in which it is written. There is no rigid system of classification for registers, as types of language are defined by their *association* with particular social situations or subject matters.

> **Register is a type of language associated with a specific social context or subject matter.**

For example, if a text uses such words and phrases as 'habeas corpus', 'heretofore', 'plaintiff' and 'judgement', we might say that it was written in a legal register. The subject matter of the text itself does not have to have anything to do with the register (although this is unusual). For instance, a children's story could feasibly be written using a legal register, although it is unlikely it would sell very well.

Most works of fiction, like most people, employ different registers at different times. This is because certain situations will be evoked and highlighted more readily by certain registers than others. A deft manipulation of register can also be used at a more fundamental level in a text. For example, in the opening paragraph of Angela Carter's *Nights at the Circus*, Fevvers uses phrases like ' "Lor' love you, sir" ' and ' "just as well 'ave" ' which belong to a rather stylized register of colloquial speech, in this case Cockney. She also mentions Venus and Helen of Troy, which belong to a more classical or mythical register. This mixture of the two registers, the colloquial and the mythical, which is maintained throughout the novel, helps to implicate the ordinary (or colloquial) in the extraordinary (or mythical) and vice versa.

## A QUICK EXERCISE

The most important thing to remember when you analyse language is just that – analyse the language, dissect the text, tear it apart word by word and show what makes it tick. Every word has a history and a context buried within it, a history and a context that alter the meaning of the words around it. Your mission, should you choose to accept it, is to unearth those contexts and histories and to show how they produce their effects.

> **Words do not exist in isolation – your job is to find the connections between them.**

Just to make sure that you have got the hang of this, try analysing the following play title. You have probably never read the play and nor do you need to know anything about it. The point of the exercise is to get you to focus at a very detailed level rather than vaguely referring to large tracts of text at once, which is what most essays do. This exercise should also help you build confidence for analysing unseen passages of text for which you will also not know the context. See how closely you can analyse it and only then compare it with my analysis. The play title is:

'MASTER HAROLD' ... *and the boys*

How did you get on? It was probably hard at first, but the trick to getting started is to break the text, or in this case the title, into its constituent parts. Here you have two terms – 'MASTER HAROLD' and *'the boys'*, joined by the conjunction *'and'*. The first term is in upper-case letters (capitals) and the second term is in lower-case letters. This suggests a relation of superiority or privilege between the two terms, in which the first term is superior to the second. This superiority is compounded by the fact that the 'master' has a name – 'Harold' – , while 'the boys' are anonymous, as if their identity is less important.

So far so good, but what about the words themselves?

- 'Master' refers to someone in control or superior to those around them, such as a school teacher. 'Master' is also the title of address for a boy. Either way, the term belongs to an old-fashioned register of speech which has connotations of the class system.
- 'The boys' refers to male children. It is also a term for men who act like children or for a group of male adult friends. In its original meaning it refers to male servants of any age, most recently black servants in the colonial system.

This complicates the previous assertion that 'MASTER HAROLD' is a privileged term over 'the boys', as both terms are ambiguous and can now refer to either adults or children.

What, then, does the fact that the first term is enclosed by quotation marks tell us? First of all it indicates that it could be a quotation, i.e., the words of another. Also, if you put quotation marks around a word it can indicate suspicion on the writer's part about the absolute validity of the term. This suggests that there is something not quite right about the term 'MASTER HAROLD'. We might propose that the respect and superiority normally accorded the term 'master' are to be treated with suspicion here. Someone is merely ventriloquizing them.

If this is the case with the first term, what about the fact that the second term, *'the boys'*, is italicized? Italics are used either to emphasize a word or phrase, or to indicate that a word or phrase is written in a foreign language. Obviously, if your native language is English, then the phrase 'and the boys' is not foreign. This therefore suggests that whomever this phrase is directed at is either not English or, at the very least, finds the term 'the boys' alien in some way.

Finally, we come to the conjunction ('and') and the ellipsis (the three dots). If we replace 'and' by 'with' we can see how the 'and' designates a much looser relationship between the two terms than 'with' would. At the most 'the boys' accompany 'Master Harold', and at worst, the 'and' signifies that they 'come after' him. This relationship is also complicated by the ellipsis. An ellipsis signifies an omission from the text, indicating that certain words have been left out. Here, the ellipsis comes between the two terms. This might suggest that the two terms can only be brought together by leaving something out or unsaid.

What, then, can we say in conclusion by rounding up all these different analyses? The typography of the title, or the way it is set out on the page, seems to indicate a relation of inequality between its two terms. The first term has a proper name and the second only warrants a generic name that is foreign or alienating. The meaning of the two terms is ambiguous, allowing either of them to be adults or boys. The meaning of the conjunction is also ambiguous, suggesting that although 'the boys' accompany 'Master Harold' they might also come after him. This relationship between the terms can finally only be maintained by leaving something unsaid.

Did you get all that? If I told you that 'MASTER HAROLD' ... *and the boys* is an excellent play by Athol Fugard depicting the relationship between a white boy and his parents' two black servants in apartheid South Africa, you might begin to see how the above analysis relates to the rest of the play.

**Always ask yourself:**
- ✔ What difference does it make using this particular word or set of words instead of another similar word or set of words?
- ✔ What are the connotations of a particular word or set of words?
- ✔ What register, or registers, is the text written in?

*Take a look at these three essay questions. 'In what ways does Act 3 Scene 1 contribute to the overall meaning of Shakespeare's Hamlet?' 'How does Iris Murdoch's The Bell treat the relationship between sexuality and spirituality?' 'Choose any three poems from Adrienne Rich's Selected Poems and consider to what extent Rich's concerns are universal concerns.' Although these questions are different in many ways, they all share a focus on a single aspect of their respective texts – themes. After 'character', 'theme' is probably the concept you are most used to dealing with in your analyses of novels and plays, and in terms of poetry it is perhaps the dominant tool in your analytical kit-bag. So if I asked you to define a theme you wouldn't have any difficulty in doing so – right?*

## WHAT IS A THEME?

A theme is an idea or topic. In literature a theme is the abstract subject of a text. For example, justice is a theme of Arthur Miller's *The Crucible*, time is a theme of Philip Larkin's *The Whitsun Weddings*, and totalitarianism is a theme of George Orwell's *Nineteen Eighty-Four*. What you might notice about these examples is that they are all abstract nouns. They refer to ideas or concepts rather than actual or material things. So, for example, if I wrote that the court gavel is a theme of Arthur Miller's *The Crucible*, the clock on the mantelpiece is a theme of Philip Larkin's *The Whitsun Weddings*, and Winston's bedroom light-bulb is a theme of George Orwell's *Nineteen Eighty-Four* you would rightly suspect I had got it wrong. This is because hammers, clocks and light-bulbs are concrete nouns, referring to things too specific to constitute a theme.

> **A theme is an idea or concept, rather than an actual or material thing.**

It is also worth noting that a single text can have a number of themes in it and is not merely restricted to one. For example, personal liberty is just as much a theme of *The Crucible* as justice is. Equally, themes do not have to be restricted to single words or abstract nouns. For example, it would probably be more accurate to state that the repressive nature of totalitarian regimes, rather than just totalitarianism, is the dominant theme of *Nineteen Eighty-Four*.

## DO I FIND A THEME OR DO I CREATE IT?

Even if you know what a theme is, how do you know where to find it? Very few texts actually declare what their themes are. Some texts do include a form of self-commentary, such as Henry Fielding's *Tom Jones* or Luigi Pirandello's *Six Characters in Search of an Author*, but even texts like these rarely state explicitly that 'Such-and-such is the theme of my work'. So how do we know, for example, that the suffusion of the spiritual and the sensual is a theme of D.H. Lawrence's *The Rainbow* and that totalitarianism is not?

The answer to this question lies in the way that themes work. Themes are the expression of a relationship between the general and the specific. They are a generalization from particular objects, characters, images or scenes. This may sound rather complicated, but a few examples will make it a lot clearer. So, Fido is a *particular* instance of the *general* class of all dogs. Roses are a *specific* form of the *general* category of flowers. Tom Cruise is a *particular* example of the *general* phenomenon of Hollywood film stars.

In literature the same relationship between the general and the particular holds true, except that the *general* is called a theme rather than a class, a category or a phenomenon. So, for example, when Darcy proposes to Elizabeth in Jane Austen's *Pride and Prejudice* it is a *specific* example of the *theme* of marriage in the novel. When Willie, in Robert Burns's 'Holy Willie's Prayer', asks God to hear him but ignore his enemies' prayers it is a *particular* instance of the poem's *general theme* of hypocrisy. Blanche's desire to return to the plantation land of Belle Reve in Tennessee Williams's *A Streetcar Named Desire* is a *specific* illustration of the *theme* of the power of dreams over reality in the play.

As themes are generalizations, this means that you must be able to point to at least two examples of a theme for it to be a theme in the first place. For example, a single description of a church does not make religion a theme in a particular text. However, if, in addition to the single description of a church, one of the main characters is a priest, there are several important confessions, and a number of metaphors which refer to the stations of the Cross, then religion, or Catholicism at least, becomes a theme of the text. This is because the setting, the character, the scenes and the imagery can all be connected with the concept of religion. There is, to put it another way, sufficient evidence or justification for religion being a theme in this text.

> **A theme is only a valid theme if you can cite several examples of it in a text.**

When you analyse a text, then, and are deciding whether or not a concept is a theme, one of the main tests for this is precisely the number of examples you can account for with that theme. For instance, if I said that playing cards is a theme in 'Holy Willie's Prayer' I would be wrong because there is only one illustration of this in the poem. This specific case is not generalizable throughout Burns's poem. The reason that I can say hypocrisy is a theme in 'Holy Willie's Prayer' is because I can find at least two examples of it in the poem, one of which is his claim to be a guide and an example to others while confessing to several sins, and another might be his chiding of Hamilton for drinking when he admits to being drunk the previous Friday. In other words, I can make a generalization about the poem. This generalization is a theme.

Those of you who have read Chapter 4 of this book will perhaps detect a similarity between making a well-connected argument and discerning a theme in a text. In fact, just as a good argument connects a large number of a text's features with each other, a good theme does likewise. The bigger the theme is, the more examples of it you can find in the text. If a theme is big enough, it will incorporate other themes within it and they will become instances of which it is a generalization. For example, in Shakespeare's *Macbeth* disease is a theme and evilness is a theme because there are plenty of examples of both throughout the play. Disease and evilness are both examples of corruption. Disease is a corruption of the health of a body and evilness is a corruption of the moral order. We can therefore say that corruption is the bigger theme in *Macbeth*.

So, to return to the question posed at the top of this section, do you *find* that corruption is a theme in *Macbeth* or do you *create* the theme yourself? The answer is a bit of both. Texts do not declare their themes, but they do contain the examples or particular instances of those themes. When you analyse a text, your job is to generalize about those particular features of a text in terms of a theme. In other words, you turn them into examples, examples of a theme. We are finally in a position, then, to schematize the construction of a theme like this:

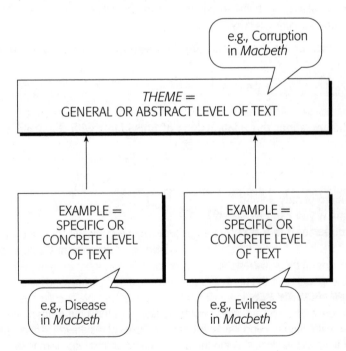

As you can see from the diagram, the value of themes resides in their ability to unify a text. Themes join together disparate features of a text, providing the text with a wholeness or unity it would otherwise lack. In this particular case,

> **The value of a theme resides in its ability to join up disparate features of a text.**

two separate features of *Macbeth* – the images of disease and evilness – are joined together by the theme of corruption.

## THE MOST COMMON THEMES

Certain themes recur from text to text, from genre to genre, and from epoch to epoch. There are two good reasons for this. One is that these themes have an abiding relevance. For example, the relationship between men and women is an enduring theme, if only because of the need to reproduce our species. A theme like this is treated very differently from text to text, but at a very general level it maintains a universal interest. The second reason that some themes are more common than others is that they are so abstract, examples of them can usually be found in most texts. For instance, while kingship is a theme of little relevance today, politics – if we interpret it broadly as the division of power – is a theme with an application across most epochs and most texts which can include more minor themes like kingship within it.

The most common themes can be roughly divided between two kinds – themes about *the relationship between an individual and the world* and themes about *the relationships of individuals with themselves*:

- **Themes about the relationship between an individual and the world** These themes deal with the interaction between individuals and the world they inhabit. Such themes might include those that deal with the connections between peoples, such as politics, history and science, and those that treat of the connections between individuals, such as sex, love and revenge.
- **Themes about the relationships of individuals with themselves** These themes deal with the interaction between an individual, whether a character or a poetic consciousness, and his or her self. Such themes might include any of the autobiographical subsets, like desire, death and artistic creation, as well as more generalized themes, such as change and how we know what we know, which have become more popular since the advent of the last century.

As you can see, these themes are neither exclusive nor water-tight, but if you are ever stuck for a theme try applying one of these categories to the text you are analysing for a bit of inspiration.

## WRITING ABOUT THEMES

When you write about a theme your basic task is to trace the route between the general – the theme – and the particular – examples of that theme. It is not enough to say that 'such-and-such' is the theme of a particular text; you also need to show how that conclusion can be reached by citing examples and demonstrating the connection between them. Let me show you what I mean. The following is an extract from an essay answering the question 'How is the relationship between private life and public life represented in Shakespeare's *Hamlet*?'

The theme of private life versus public life is manifest in all the spying that takes place in *Hamlet*. For example, when Hamlet speaks to his mother in her bedchamber he is being spied upon by

> **When you write about themes you need to trace the connection between a theme and its examples.**

Polonius and, in turn, the Ghost of the King. Conversely, when Claudius is at prayer, Hamlet spies on him. Also, at the beginning of Act 3 Scene 1 Claudius and Polonius spy on Hamlet so that, 'Seeing unseen', they may check on his state of mind. This spying gives rise to counter-surveillance. If we look at the missing stage direction from Quarto 1 – 'Enter Hamlet *reading a book*' – we suspect that the 'To be or not to be' soliloquy is in fact a ruse. Hamlet acts out a moment of introspection in order to mislead Claudius and Polonius because he either knows they are watching or expects they might be. The consequence of this for the theme of private life versus public life is that there is no private life. All the spying in the play puts private lives under surveillance and makes them public.

Can you see how this essay has demonstrated the validity of a theme here? The paragraph begins by stating the main theme, that of the relationship between public and private life, and making the claim that a subset of this is the theme of spying. In order to prove that spying is indeed a theme, the essay cites several examples of spying in the play. Having validated the theme of spying, the essay goes on to connect this to the larger theme, claiming that all the surveillance in *Hamlet* turns private lives into public ones. In other words, the essay does not directly move from

> **Always try to break down a large theme into its subsets in order to demonstrate the nuances of a text.**

the larger theme (private versus public) to the text, but demonstrates that this movement is mediated by smaller themes (in this case, spying). This is a good tactic to employ when writing about themes because if you can break down a big theme into its subsets you show an appreciation of the subtleties and nuances of a text which will help increase your grade.

**Always ask yourself:**
- ✔ Is the theme I am writing about an idea or merely a thing which is not really a theme?
- ✔ Are there enough examples in the text to prove that the theme I am writing about really is a theme rather than an isolated idea?
- ✔ Are there any subsets of the theme I am writing about?

## 10

# Analysing grammar

*Can you tell the difference between an adjective and an adverb? Or between a conjunction and a preposition? Would you know how to divide up a sentence between its subject, object and verb? If you can't, you are not alone. Many students find it difficult to distinguish between the different categories of language with sufficient accuracy. In order to overcome that problem, this chapter is designed to provide you with a basic knowledge of grammar and to show you how to analyse it.*

### BUT WHY DO I NEED TO KNOW ABOUT GRAMMAR? IT'S SO BORING!

Grammar can be defined in many different ways, but for the purposes of writing A-Level essays, grammar needs to be understood in two principal modes:

- **It is the system of abstract rules which govern the correct use of a language.** This aspect of grammar mainly affects the actual writing of essays. If you do not understand these rules you will not be able to write properly and you will be marked down accordingly. The chances are that you have an intuitive grasp of most of these rules already. However, if you are able to articulate them more explicitly then you will be able to recognize and explain how certain texts bend the rules to achieve certain effects.
- **It is a system of classification by which we name the different parts of our language.** This aspect of grammar mainly affects how you analyse a text. You need to be able to name the different grammatical units and explain how their use produces specific effects. Too many essays contain such imprecise descriptions as, 'This story is written in simple language', 'This poem has many airy-fairy words in it', or, 'The narrator uses long sentences'. It is therefore the case that when a student manages to employ the correct technical terms with which to describe a piece of prose, drama or poetry, he or she will gain not only in precision, but in grade too.

If you think of grammar as merely a system of rules and names, then it might very well seem boring. However, if you are also able to appreciate that in applying these rules and names you open up the text to whole new areas of analysis, you can see how the study of grammar becomes a lot more interesting. Specifically, you realize that by employing

> **If you analyse the grammar of a text you will greatly increase your chances of a higher grade because most students simply ignore it.**

and analysing grammatical concepts within your essay you can dramatically improve your grade.

## BASIC GRAMMATICAL UNITS

### Noun

A word that refers to a person, thing or place, e.g. woman, lamp, country. Nouns can be classified further according to whether they are:

* *concrete* nouns (designating actual or material things, e.g. a potato, a book, a post)
* *abstract* nouns (referring to ideas or concepts, e.g. hope, faith, charity)
* *proper* nouns (names of specific people or places, e.g. France, Alison, The Beatles)
* *common* nouns (designating general types of nouns, e.g. cars, apples, planets)

The relative frequency with which particular noun types are used can tell you a lot about a text. For example, Nick Carraway, the narrator of F. Scott Fitzgerald's *The Great Gatsby*, employs an unusually high proportion of abstract nouns, e.g. 'promise', 'ideal', 'spirit' and so forth. This helps to signify his concern with spiritual or moral matters and thus partly explains both his support for the dreamer Gatsby, and his contempt for the more materialistic Tom, who makes correspondingly greater use of concrete nouns.

### Pronoun

A word which stands in for a noun that has been already mentioned, or is about to be mentioned, e.g. it, this, that. One of the more common grammatical errors to be found in essays occurs when a pronoun is employed either with reference to a noun that was mentioned several sentences earlier, or with reference to a noun that is not mentioned at all. For example, the sentence 'He went left and then he went right' makes little sense unless we know who 'he' is. If you wrote 'Stuart went left and then he went right' instead, then the reader knows that the pronoun 'he' refers to 'Stuart'.

### Verb

A word that indicates an action, e.g. run, sing, dance. It is perhaps not too much of a generalization to say that verbs have, over the past hundred years, come to dominate writing at the expense of adverbs and adjectives. This is partly because a higher frequency of verb use creates an impression of activity, energy and movement which helps to reflect the rapid pace of change in the modern world.

In terms of essay writing, you may wish to know that it is considered to be a minor form of heresy by some teachers if you split the infinitive form of a verb ('to *something*', e.g. to run, to sing, to dance). Putting aside the perennial argument over whether English actually has infinitives, this merely means that you do not insert a word between 'to' and the verb, e.g. 'to gladly hear' is wrong, but 'to hear gladly' is right.

## Verb tense

The tense of a verb refers to its temporal mode, or inflection, e.g. past, present and future. The relevance of verb tense for literary studies is that it expresses a relation between the time when something is told and the time when it happened. Most prose works, for example, are written in the past tense. This indicates that the tales they are telling have already happened and that the story is moving to a predefined point before the present of the telling. In such cases, you know that, for instance, the narrator will not expire before the end of the story. If, on the other hand, a narrative is written in the present tense, such as Bobbie Ann Mason's 'Shiloh', this indicates that the story is being told at the same time that it is happening. This creates a sense of undecidability as to what will happen which, in the case of 'Shiloh', helps to portray the theme of the difficulty of coping with the uncertainty of change.

> **Always write your essay in the present rather than the past tense.**

## Verb mood

The mood of a verb indicates the type of character the verb has. There are three basic moods in the English language: the indicative, the imperative and the subjunctive.

- The **indicative** is the most common verb mood. It is used to state a fact or question. For example, in the sentence 'John chops the wood', 'chops' is in the indicative mood. In the sentence 'I am analysing the text', 'analysing' is in the indicative mood. In the sentence 'He wept at his essay's mark', 'wept' is in the indicative mood.
- The **imperative** is the second most common verb mood. It is used to command or request someone to do something. For example, in the sentence 'Chop the wood!', 'chop' is in the imperative mood. In the sentence 'Analyse the text!', 'analyse' is in the imperative mood. In the sentence 'Weep at your essay mark!', 'weep' is in the imperative mood. As you might have noticed here, the imperative always takes the second person (singular or plural) of the verb form, that is 'You do something'. It is also very often indicated by an exclamation mark.
- The **subjunctive** is the least common verb mood. It is used to express doubts, wishes or fears about something which is contrary to fact or does not yet exist in reality. For example, in the sentence 'If there were any trees, I would chop the wood', 'were' is in the subjunctive mood. In the sentence 'I suggest that the text be analysed', 'be' is in the subjunctive. In the sentence 'I wish I didn't weep at my essay mark', 'didn't' is in the subjunctive mood. As you can see from these examples, the rules for the subjunctive vary enormously, but, as a basic guide, if something is not being asserted or commanded and is a matter of speculation then it is in the subjunctive.

If you think of verb moods as existing on a continuum, the indicative is the neutral term and the subjunctive and the imperative make up either end:

| Subjunctive | Indicative | Imperative |

The Verb Mood Continuum

Perhaps one of the most useful applications of the verb mood continuum is in the analysis of characterization in literature. It is possible to plot the development of characters using the continuum, connecting different verb moods to changes in their outlook or position. For example, Thomas Gradgrind in Charles Dickens's *Hard Times* adopts the indicative mood as something of a philosophy. Throughout the majority of the novel he bullies the other characters with his imperative cry of 'Give me the facts, just the facts!' However, upon realizing he has ruined his children's lives, he becomes more open-minded and starts speculating on what might have been. This marks his transition to the subjunctive mood. Conversely, it might be said of Hamlet, in Shakespeare's *Hamlet*, that he spends most of the play in the subjunctive mood plagued by doubts over what he should and could do. However, at the end of the play his language becomes more indicative as he resolves to act and avenge his father's murder.

> **You can trace the development of characters to changes in the predominant use of a particular verb mood.**

The injunctions and exclamations of the pilgrims in Chaucer's *Canterbury Tales* or the judgements on the characters and directions to the reader of William Thackeray's *Vanity Fair* all belong to the imperative or the subjunctive moods. These techniques were commonplace during the times in which these works were written but they are rare now. Instead, modern literature tends to be written in the indicative mood, a technique perfected in works like Albert Camus's *The Outsider* or Samuel Beckett's *Waiting for Godot*. In texts such as these, the indicative mood is used to reflect an alienation or distance from the world – no wishes are

> **In modern literature the indicative mood has come to predominate over the imperative and subjunctive moods.**

expressed, no judgements are passed, no orders are given, rather, everything just *is*.

### Adverb
A word that modifies the meaning of a verb or sentence, e.g. very, sadly, probably.

### Adjective
A word which conveys a characteristic of a noun or pronoun, e.g. adhesive, deaf, pithy. As I have already mentioned, adjectives and adverbs have suffered a relative decline in use over the past hundred years. This is because they are thought to 'hold up' the action of a narrative. If you think of a story as a journey, then verbs signify a forward movement, while adjectives and adverbs constitute a little detour around a

cul-de-sac. Contemporary plot-centred popular fiction employs a lower frequency of adjectives and adverbs than the canonical English Literature of the type you will be more likely to study. The higher frequency of adjectival and adverbial use in this latter category makes it easier for you to write the kind of essays which make connections and establish significances between different parts of a text.

### Preposition
A word used with a noun or pronoun to relate it to another part of the sentence, e.g. for, to, at. It is worth knowing that many teachers think that it is the devil's own work if you end a sentence with a preposition.

### Conjunction
A word that connects words, phrases or clauses in a sentence, e.g. and, but, while. Some teachers will stop speaking to you if you begin a sentence with a conjunction.

### Subject, object and predicate
The subject of a verb is the one undertaking the action, while the object of a verb is the one to whom the verb is being done. In the phrase 'the boy caught the ball', 'the boy' is the subject of the verb ('to catch') and 'the ball' is the object. A sentence can also be split up between a subject and a predicate. The predicate is that part of a sentence which asserts or denies something about the subject of a sentence. In the phrase 'the boy caught the ball', 'caught the ball' is the predicate.

At the heart of every proper sentence is a **simple subject** and a **simple predicate**. The simple subject is the subject of the verb shorn of all its qualifying adjec-

> **A proper sentence contains a subject and a predicate (usually containing a verb and an object).**

tives. The simple predicate is the verb shorn of all its qualifying adverbs. For example, in the sentence 'Poor, disheartened Kathryn, very wearily and very slowly, walked to her maths class', 'Kathryn' is the simple subject and 'walked' is the simple predicate. In other words, stripped down, the bare facts of the sentence are that 'Kathryn walked'. Clearly, the statement that 'Kathryn walked' tells you very little. The real information, concerning Kathryn's state of mind as she approaches her class, is contained in the non-essential parts of the sentence – those bits outside of the simple subject and the simple predicate.

As a general rule, this also holds true for literature. The patterns you are looking for when you analyse a text tend to be found in those words left over when you have stripped a sentence down to its simple subject and predicate. If you are stuck

> **If you are stuck, try stripping down a sentence to its simple subject and predicate and looking at what is left over.**

when analysing a text, then one technique you might try is to identify the simple subject and predicate of a sentence and look at what's left over.

Take the first sentence of Mary Shelley's *Frankenstein*, for example: 'You will rejoice to hear that no disaster has accompanied the commencement of an enterprise which you have regarded with such evil forebodings'. In this sentence the simple subject is 'you'. There are two predicates here – 'will rejoice' and 'have regarded'. When there are two or more predicates in a sentence they combine to form a **compound** predicate. Stripped down, the sentence basically states that 'you will rejoice' and 'you have regarded'. The real significance of the sentence, however, lies in what is left out of the bare facts, the ominous words 'disaster', 'evil' and 'fore-bodings'. These words, rather than the compound predicate, foreshadow the horror of Frankenstein's project as it unfolds in the rest of the book.

**Always ask yourself:**
- ✔ Have I identified the different grammatical components of a text?
- ✔ Have I analysed the effects of the arrangement of the different grammatical components of a text?
- ✔ Have I followed the rules of grammar in writing my essay?

## 11

# Analysing rhetoric

*Can you tell the difference between a simile and a metaphor? Or between a hyperbole and a euphemism? Would you know how to distinguish a symbol from an allegory? You certainly need to be able to if you are going to get a good grade for your essays. This chapter is designed to help you identify these figures of speech, to provide you with a basic knowledge of rhetoric and to show you how to analyse it.*

## WHAT IS RHETORIC?

Rhetoric is the study of the technique of writing and speaking effectively. As a discipline it was originally developed by Classical theoreticians to explain how to create persuasive orations. It centres around units of speech called 'rhetorical figures'. These units are now more commonly termed 'figures of speech'.

There are about 350 rhetorical figures, many of which, such as 'example' and 'dilemma', have passed into common usage. Luckily, you do not need to know all of these. However, every exam board not only expects you to be able to name

> **The exam boards give you extra marks if you can name and analyse rhetorical figures correctly.**

and analyse the most frequently used figures of speech but will give you extra marks for doing so.

## BASIC RHETORICAL UNITS

### Metaphor

A figure of speech used to designate a resemblance in qualities between one person or thing and another person and thing, e.g. 'he is a mountain of a man'. Metaphors are constructed from two parts – the tenor and the vehicle. The tenor of a metaphor is its subject, in this case 'the man'. The vehicle of a metaphor is the word to which the subject, or tenor, of the metaphor is being implicitly compared in quality, so in this case it is 'mountain'. In the metaphor, 'my tears are a sea', 'tears' is the tenor and 'sea' is the vehicle.

### Simile

A figure of speech used to make an explicit comparison between one person or thing and another person or thing, e.g. 'that man is like a mountain'.

> **Similes always contain the words 'like' or 'as', whereas metaphors do not.**

Both metaphors and similes have fallen into relative disfavour over recent years for the same reasons that adverbs and adjectives have. They are considered to be a form of ornamentation, not really necessary to the real function of telling the story. This, of course, is pure nonsense, as the more 'poetical' aspects of language are the ones that enable it to produce significance. If, for example, I write, 'my tears' it will tell you nothing beyond the fact that I have tears. It is the same as writing 'my tears are my tears'. If, however, I write, 'my tears are like a sea' it will provide you with some kind of understanding of the qualities of my tears, or in this case, the quantity of them. Metaphors and similes should thus be one of your first ports of

> **Metaphors and similes indicate the value and significance of what is being described.**

call when you analyse a text as they will help you to determine the significance and value of what is being described.

### Symbol

A symbol is something which represents something else, usually by convention or association, e.g. roses are a conventional symbol for love, white is a symbol of innocence and skulls are a symbol of death. Symbols are a type of metaphor in which the subject, or tenor, of the metaphor is omitted, leaving only the vehicle. This means that symbols are often difficult to interpret as you can never be 100 per cent certain what the hidden tenor might be. How, then, do you recognize a symbol?

The key to recognizing a symbol is convention. Many symbols can be recognized because they are conventionally treated as symbols. Skulls are an habitual symbol of death, for instance. Nevertheless, not every skull is a symbol; it all depends upon the context in which the skull features. A skull may be thought of as a symbol, only if it is referred to in a way that suggests it has more significance than just being a skull. Thus, for example, when Hamlet picks up Yorick's skull and starts talking about his childhood, the skull becomes a symbol of the loss of his happy and innocent young life. If, on the other hand, Hamlet just picked up Yorick's skull and started talk-

> **The key to recognizing a symbol is convention.**

ing about its nice bone structure, he would be treating it as a skull and nothing else.

Many symbols are less obvious, however, because the majority of authors, dramatists and poets like either to create their own symbols or to adapt ones from the common stock. When this happens, though, the same rules still apply: *a word becomes a symbol when it is repeatedly treated as if it means more than it actually denotes.*

> **A word becomes a symbol when it is repeatedly treated as if it means more than it actually denotes.**

If you now know how to recognize a symbol, how do you know if you are interpreting it properly? The trick here is once again to take account of the context in which it occurs. If, for example, you propose that when Hamlet picks up Yorick's skull he is using it as a symbol of the extraordinary success of McDonald's restaurants you are clearly mistaken. McDonald's had yet to be invented at the time of Shakespeare's writing the play, there is no reference to burgers in the play, and Hamlet does not address these concerns when he transforms the skull into a symbol. In other words, you can produce no justification for your interpretation.

As soon as you are able to justify your interpretation of a word as a symbol, you have found a 'proper' interpretation of it. This does not mean that there is only one way to interpret a symbol. Indeed, symbols are used precisely because they afford the reader a certain degree of flexibility in interpretation. So, as long as you can support your analysis with evidence from the text, then you have interpreted it 'properly'.

### Allegory

I suspect that one of the reasons students have difficulties with symbols generally, and why, in particular, they tend to 'find' symbols where there are none, is because of the popularity of George Orwell's classic novels *Animal Farm* and *Nineteen Eighty-Four* as school teaching books. Both these stories have notorious subtexts and they therefore tend to foster a certain attitude towards studying literature which involves searching for hidden' meanings. However, these texts and others like them, including John Bunyan's *Pilgrim's Progress*, Jonathan Swift's *Gulliver's Travels*, Edmund Spenser's *The Faerie Queene* and Dante's *Divine Comedy*, are more conventionally described as being *allegorical*, rather than symbolic.

An allegory is like a symbol, in that it is a metaphor in which the tenor is missing and only the vehicle is visible. However, unlike a symbol, the missing tenor is usually quite specific and you therefore do not have the same freedom of interpretation that you do when analysing a symbol. Furthermore, and particularly with modern allegorical works, it is not always clear that a text is an allegory as there tend to be fewer clues to its allegorical status than there would be if it were a symbolic work. This is because the vehicle of an allegory – which is usually the whole work – tends to form a proper, discrete story all by itself. You will very often only know when a text is allegorical if you are told that it is.

**An allegory is a symbol with a specific tenor.**

Some works, like *Pilgrim's Progress*, are clearly allegorical, but my advice is that you do not treat a work as having an allegorical, or overall, 'hidden', meaning unless you are told to do so. Allegory is not, and has not been, a popular form of writing in English for hundreds of years. There are two main reasons for this. The first is that allegory was part of the Christian tradition in which the divine purpose of God was revealed in human history, and as that tradition has waned in influence, so has the relevance of allegory. The second reason is that the harsh political conditions preceding democracy, which meant that writers had to conceal the true, controversial meaning of their texts, are no longer in place. You will therefore tend to find that contemporary allegorical works are only produced in countries with oppressive regimes and strong censorship.

## Metonymy

A figure of speech where an attribute or feature of a person or thing is substituted for the thing itself, e.g. 'the crown' represents the monarchy, 'the bottle' stands in for alcoholic drink, 'the reds' refers to communists.

The use of metonymy is often very subtle. For example, the phrase 'the bustling street' may be used as a metonym for crowded city pavements, where transactions are undertaken in shops, business deals are struck, pick-pockets are in operation, people are talking, walking, shouting, and so on. In other words, a metonym allows an author to delete a vast quantity of description by implying rather than describing something. It has thus experienced a resurgence in popularity over recent years, at the expense of metaphor, because it allows the author to keep up the pace of a story without taking a detour into description.

> **Metonymy is used to represent vast scenes in a small number of words.**

## Hyperbole

An exaggeration which adds emphasis to an expression, e.g. 'A million years later the lesson came to an end'. Hyperbole generally works by contrasting the actual state of affairs with the emotional experience of that state of affairs. Often, therefore, it imparts a sense of comedy, as the discrepancy between what is being described and what is felt can be enormous. Nevertheless, it can be used for other effects.

During the graveyard quarrel between Hamlet and Laertes in *Hamlet*, for example, the characters engage in a hyperbolic duel over who can create the biggest mountains of earth over Ophelia's grave. The hyperbole here works in many ways. It foreshadows the actual duel between Hamlet and Laertes, signifies the inexpressible depth of their grief at her death, and illustrates the dangerous level of hysteria occasioned by that sadness. Furthermore, as hyperbole is a personal response to an objective situation it tends to display a rather egocentric view of the world. This, it may be argued, is at work in this scene, where Hamlet and Laertes seem more concerned with themselves than with the fate of Ophelia.

## Euphemism

A figure of speech which allows an inoffensive expression to be used in place of an offensive, explicit or otherwise alarming phrase. For example, 'sleep with' is a euphemism for 'have sexual intercourse with', while 'passed on' is a euphemism for 'died'.

## Parataxis

Short, pithy sentences that either contain no clauses or omit the use of conjunctions, e.g. 'the boy caught the ball – it was green'. This is often what students mean when they describe a text as 'simple'. It is a type of phrasing popular with contemporary politicians, but also with authors such as Ernest Hemingway and Kurt Vonnegut.

## Hypotaxis

Long sentences that contain many clauses and frequent use of conjunctions. This is the opposite of parataxis, although they are very often used together in order to provide contrast and highlight the meaning of their respective sentences. In its pure form, such as that practised by Henry James and Joseph Conrad, one sentence can seem to run for several pages, taking in so many pronouns that by the end of it you have no idea what the sentence was about. Savour those moments – they mean you are not alone.

## Irony

This is a form of writing or speaking where you declare one thing but actually mean another. Like symbolism, irony works by referring to something that is not actually explicit in the text. Whether or not you perceive that a statement is ironic, therefore, depends upon your knowledge of the context in which it is made.

A quick glance at the most famous ironic statement in English Literature – the opening sentence of Jane Austen's *Pride and Prejudice* – should make this clear: 'It is a truth universally acknowledged that a single man in possession of a good fortune must be in want of a wife'. We know this is ironic for several reasons. Our first clue can be found in the phrase 'universally acknowledged' and the imperative expression of the word 'must'. Both of these make an explicit appeal to a common set of values – a set of values that it is unlikely either we, or, as it turns out, the single men in possession of good fortune in the novel share. The 'truth' of the assertion is therefore not 'universal'; it is, rather, a limited truth held, as we find out, only by those women in the novel who want to marry into money. The statement is ironic, therefore, because it adopts the view-point of these characters and pretends it is universal in the knowledge that this is only a minority point of view. The narrator's statement, in other words, relies for its ironic effect upon an *implicit* appeal to a common set of values – a set of values in which it is *not* universally acknowledged that single men in possession of a good fortune are in want of a wife.

Most irony works in this way by appealing to a shared set of assumptions, an appeal which is very often signposted

> **Irony works by appealing to a muted but shared set of assumptions.**

by phrases like 'of course', 'no more than natural', 'universally acknowledged', etc. Over time and across cultures, ironic statements tend to lose their effectiveness. If I wrote that 'Of course witches should not be burned', then the chances are you would agree with me. If I had written that in the tenth century, the chances are that you would have thought I was being ironic (unless you were a witch) because it

> **Over time and across cultures, irony tends to lose its effectiveness.**

was commonly assumed that witches should be burned. When you are writing about irony in a text, you need to explain exactly why a statement is ironic by demonstrating how the statement makes an appeal to a set of values either explicit in the text or implicit in the community of readers.

**Always ask yourself:**
✔ Have I identified the different rhetorical components of a text?
✔ Have I analysed the effects of the arrangement of the different rhetorical components of a text?
✔ Have I produced evidence to back up my claim for hidden meanings in the text?

# Analysing structure

## 12

*Most students are happy to write about the characters and themes of a text, or what might be called the content of a text, but they feel less comfortable writing about a text's structure, or what is sometimes referred to as its form. If you write about the structure of a text, you stand a substantial chance of increasing your grade. Which raises the question, what exactly is 'structure'? The structure of a novel, poem or play is the conceptual framework upon which it is built. If this sounds rather complicated, think of it as the paraphrase of a story in terms of ideas, rather than in terms of plot. When you describe the structure of a poem, novel or play you are doing no more than summarizing its story in the abstract. If you are still not sure what this means, the rest of this chapter will illustrate some of the more common types of structure to be found in literature.*

## THE SIMPLEST STRUCTURE OF THEM ALL

The most common and at the same time the simplest structure of them all is the one where a conflict is resolved. It can be written schematically like this:

Conflict —————→ Resolution

All this type of structure requires is that there be at least two parties, that these two parties enter into a state of discord and that this discord is somehow resolved. The parties involved can be anyone, from two characters to the split mind of an individual; the conflict can be about anything, from ideas to physical superiority; and its resolution can take any form from a harmonious agreement to the total destruction of one of the parties involved. Sophocles' *Antigone*, for example, is centred upon the *conflict* between Creon and Antigone concerning the right way to bury Antigone's brother, and it is *resolved* when Antigone dies and Creon relents, burying her brother properly.

In fact, almost all texts have this kind of structure hidden within them: two parties are introduced, conflict with each other, and somehow resolve that conflict. Here are some examples:

- Henry Fielding's *Tom Jones* centres upon a conflict between the rights of blood and the rights of individual merit which is resolved when Tom, who represents the latter, marries Sophia.
- Andrew Marvell's *A Dialogue between the Resolved Soul and Created Pleasure* revolves around the conflict between the pleasure of immediate gratification

and the delights of a heavenly eternity. This is resolved when it is found that the former pleasures are but a limited example of the latter delights.

- Henrik Ibsen's *A Doll's House* is about the conflict between the independence of women and the subservience of women to men and it is resolved in favour of the former when Nora leaves Thorvald and sets up life on her own.

Looking at a text in terms of the conflict-resolution model will help you to clarify your understanding of it. As a general rule, you can interpret characters in regard to the ideas they represent. For example, in F. Scott Fitzgerald's *Tender is the Night* Nicole broadly represents materialism and Dick broadly represents idealism. Furthermore, in most texts one character tends to finish ahead of the others, whether that is expressed as killing the other character or merely having the last word. This roughly means that the idea which that character represents is victorious. So, in the case of *Tender is the Night*, Nicole has the last word and Dick fades into obscurity, which means that the conflict between materialism and idealism is resolved in favour of the former. As I say, this is only a rough and ready type of analysis, but in the early stages of planning your essay it will help you to clarify the issues involved.

> **The last character left standing tends to be the one in whose favour the conflict is resolved.**

It is also worth noting that the particular manner in which the conflict is resolved will help you to classify the type of structure of the text you are studying. The most common types of resolution are *death* and *marriage*. Texts ending in death are often described as tragedies, while texts ending in marriages are often described as comedies.

## BINARY OPPOSITIONS

Analysing structure depends upon discerning the way in which different concepts are put into conflict with each other. One way of doing this is to set out the conflict in terms of a table of binary oppositions. A binary opposition is simply a pair of related terms in which one has a positive value and the other a negative value. These values are assigned in response to the way the text treats the opposing terms. For example, *day/night* and *sun/moon* are two sets of binary oppositions in Bram Stoker's *Dracula*. The former of each pair has a positive value and the latter of each pair has a negative value because, as we all know, vampires only come out at night and are afraid of the sunlight.

> **A binary opposition is a pair of related terms in which one has a positive value and the other a negative value.**

Every text is built upon a more or less explicit structure of binary oppositions. The real interest in these structures lies in the way the opposing terms are given a positive or negative value by a text and whether or not those values change during the course of the text. So, for example, at the beginning of *Antigone*, Creon is a king and Antigone is an outlaw. We may therefore provisionally assign a positive value to Creon (as he occupies a socially acceptable position in the play) and a negative value to Antigone (as she occupies a socially unacceptable position in the play), allowing us to create the following table:

| + | − |
|---|---|
| Creon | Antigone |

Having set up these initial terms, we may then add to them by noting other terms that the play allies with either of the oppositions. For example, considerable emphasis is laid upon the fact that Antigone is merely a woman, that she wishes to bury her dead brother in contradistinction to the law, and that she wishes to do so because it is respectful to the gods. We might therefore add the following terms to our table:

| + | − |
|---|---|
| Creon | Antigone |
| Man | Woman |
| Law | Family |
| The State | The Gods |
| The Living | The Dead |

We are now in a position to understand *Antigone* as a conflict between certain themes and values. The conflict is resolved when the system of oppositions collapses – what in the case of Greek tragedy we might call the *peripetia* or reversal. Towards the end of *Antigone*, then, Creon is compared to a woman, he forgives his niece, buries the dead properly and learns to accept the rule of the gods over the state. In other words, all the terms associated with Antigone finally prove triumphant and we can see that our initial ascription of a negative value to her was wrong. On this reading, therefore, we can say that the underlying structure of the play is one that ends up positively valuing women, the family, the dead, and, of course, the gods, despite the fact that at the level of the plot Antigone is an outlaw condemned to death.

## TRIANGULAR STRUCTURES
One of the more common variations of the kind of binary structures discussed above is the triangular or ternary arrangement of a text, much beloved of the novel

in particular. The standard ternary structure of a text centres upon the eternal triangle of desire in which there are three characters, two of whom desire the third. In turn, the third character tends to find *both* of the other characters appealing, although this is not necessarily vital. Examples of such triangular relationships include Emma, Charles and Rodolphe in Gustave Flaubert's *Madame Bovary*, Gatsby, Tom and Daisy in F. Scott Fitzgerald's *The Great Gatsby*, and even Mr and Mrs Morel and their son Paul in D.H. Lawrence's *Sons and Lovers*.

What is interesting about this kind of ternary structure is that, if you look at these examples, they all involve a specific relationship between the genders in which the first two characters are male and the third one is female. More specifically these relationships tend to develop from the rivalry between the two men and, in fact, actually centre upon them rather than the woman concerned. This is why I say that this is a variation on a binary structure, because the male characters are essentially competing with each other for the female character. Such triangular structures as these, then, are generally chauvinist in character because the female character is reduced to the status of a trophy or a means of showing who has 'won' between the male characters. For example, in *Tom Jones* the real relationship is not between Tom and Sophia, but between Tom and Blifil who compete to see who can marry Sophia. The affections of Sophia thus represent no more than the positive or negative value in the binary opposition between Tom and Blifil.

> **Triangular structures are often secret binary structures in which two characters compete against each other to 'win' the third character.**

## STRUCTURES OF REPETITION

You may also have noticed that most structures involve a repetition or return to the initial conflict which set the whole play, poem or novel going in the first place. This is not necessarily a complete or pure repetition but a quasi-repetition in which the scene or line is repeated with a significant development. In Toni Morrison's *Beloved*, for example, the conflict between Sethe's present and past is only resolved when the scene where the slave-owners come to recapture her and her children is repeated, but this time with a more positive outcome. Similarly, in *The Great Gatsby*, Gatsby's conflict between the ideal and the material worlds is only resolved when he repeats his attempt to woo Daisy. In poetry such repetitions tend to take the form of variations on a refrain, as in William Blake's 'The Clod and the Pebble' where the line 'And builds a Heaven in Hell's despair' is repeated as 'And builds a Hell in Heaven's despite'.

> **Most texts are built upon a repetition in which a scene or line is repeated but with a significant change or development.**

Many authors convey this sense of repetition by employing cyclical structures to underpin their work. A good number of Shakespeare's plays, for example, are built upon a structure of recirculation in which order is established (or referred to), disorder sets in, and then order is restored. In *A Midsummer Night's Dream*, for example, the play begins by establishing the solidity of Theseus's reign. This is then thrown into disequilibrium when Lysander and Hermia contest his authority by eloping to the forest in order to escape his edict concerning her marriage. Theseus then goes to the forest – the scene of the *revolution* – where he agrees to their marriage. After that, they all troop back to the city feeling very happy and order is restored.

In this instance, the cyclical structure of the play is spatial because it involves a repetition of place. It starts in the city, moves to the forest, and then returns to the city. In other texts, a cyclical pattern might be more obviously temporal, involving the repetition of a particular time. An old favourite is to employ the seasons, which obviously always recur and return. You can see this at work in, for example, Toni Morrison's *The Bluest Eye*, which is structured around four sections – Autumn, Winter, Spring and Summer. Cyclical structures, such as those based on the seasons or the life-cycle, help to convey a sense of inevitability. For example, the terrible fate of Cholly and Pecola in *The Bluest Eye* is inevitable, or at least unsurprising, given the forces acting on their lives. The cyclical structure of the narrative underwrites

> **Cyclical structures, such as those based on the seasons or the life-cycle, help to convey a sense of inevitability.**

this inevitability along with other aspects of the novel, such as the imagery of growing plants from seeds.

## WRITING ABOUT STRUCTURE

As you can see from all of these examples, every text is structured in a number of different ways. The type of structure you write about will depend on the argument of your essay. If, for example, you are writing about male chauvinism in *The Great Gatsby* it will be more pertinent to your thesis to write about the triangular structure between Gatsby, Tom and Daisy rather than the novel's structure of repetition. On the other hand, if you are making an argument about time in the novel, Gatsby's attempt to repeat the past will be more relevant to your essay than an analysis of the novel's ternary structure. In other words, there is a degree of freedom involved in writing about structure and it is not simply a matter of right or wrong.

> **All texts are built upon a number of different structures, but the structure you write about should be the one most pertinent to your argument.**

## Always ask yourself:

✔ Is there a conflict in this text, and if so, what is about, who or what is it between and how is it resolved?

✔ Is anything repeated in this text, and if so, how does the first scene or line change in the second scene or line, and to what effect?

✔ Am I writing about the structure most relevant to my argument?

# Analysing text and context

## 13

*Until recently you may well have thought of yourself as a student of English Literature. Well, you still are, but, whether you know it or not, you are now also a student of Literary Studies. This subtle change in emphasis is the result of developments in research undertaken in Literature departments across the world. The basic difference between English Literature and Literary Studies is the difference between concentrating on the text alone and including a discussion of the context of the text in your essays. This begs the question of what exactly constitutes the 'context' of a text, so, in order to help you understand the different meanings of 'context', this chapter will explain what is meant by the term and how you can incorporate it into your essays.*

### A QUICK HISTORY OF THE STUDY OF ENGLISH LITERATURE

If we are talking about the context of literature, there can be no better place to start than the context of Literature itself. It is worth remembering in this respect that the concept of literature we have today – that is, of fictitious writing as a product of the imagination – is still relatively young, having only developed at the beginning of the nineteenth century. The study of this kind of English Literature was first undertaken at university level in 1828 at King's College, London. The impetus behind this new subject was to furnish the middle classes (mainly women) with a sense of culture and heritage and to civilize the working classes, hopefully pacifying them in the process so that they would not indulge in the revolutionary activities of their Continental counterparts. In this sense English Literature was felt to be a substitute for the failure of organized religion, which at that time was beginning its steady decline.

**Both the concept of literature, as we understand it, and the study of literature are relatively recent phenomena.**

The study of English Literature continued doubling as a poor man's Classics and moral tea-cosy until, in the 1920s, a new breed of scholars at Cambridge University revolutionized the discipline. The particular distinction of these pioneers was to convert English Literature into a distinct object of study with its own critical apparatus and terminology. They also helped to establish the canon or list of texts which are most often studied. In the space of a decade they turned English Literature into the most respectable of academic disciplines and, in the process, bequeathed later generations the method of studying texts which, in tandem with the American New Criticism, is still the most

> **The way most people study texts – Practical Criticism – was invented in the 1920s.**

influential today – Practical Criticism. The technique of Practical Criticism is quite simple – it involves studying 'the words on the page' and nothing else.

## THE CONTEXT STRIKES BACK

The Anglo-American school of literary criticism remained more or less unchallenged until the late 1960s when it began to be contested by various schools of critical thought from Continental Europe. These different schools, which are grouped together under the name of Literary Theory, differ from Anglo-American criticism in many ways, but the most basic difference is that they propose a text cannot be divorced from its context. For them, literature is not written in a vacuum or read in one, so any analysis of a text has to include a consideration of its conditions of production and reception.

> **In the 1960s Practical Criticism was challenged by Literary Theory, which argued that a text cannot be understood outside of its contexts.**

## DIFFERENT TYPES OF CONTEXT

A text can be contextualized in many different ways, but I will consider the five types of context most commonly referred to in Literary Studies – the *linguistic*, the *literary*, the *cultural*, the *political* and the *historical*.

### Linguistic context

The meaning of words changes over time and across cultures. For example, the word 'barber' has for us a straightforward meaning of 'a male hairdresser'. In Shakespeare's day, however, 'barber' not only referred to a type of hairdresser-surgeon but also had connotations of a promiscuous and effeminizing sexuality, connotations which perhaps change our understanding of the description of Antony in *Antony and Cleopatra* as being 'barber'd ten times o'er'. Words not only change over time but are often ambiguous at any particular time. When, for example, we read the first line of William Blake's 'The Sick Rose' – 'O Rose, thou art sick!' – what does 'Rose' actually refer to here? Is the poem's persona addressing a flower-bed, a person or a pet called Rose, a person who bears a physical resemblance to a rose, or someone whose characteristics are matched by the connotations of the flower?

> **The meaning of a word not only changes over time and across cultures, but has different connotations for different people.**

### Literary context

Poets, dramatists and authors write their works under the influence of previously written literature. This influence can take different forms. At a basic level, there are certain expectations about the type of genre to which a text belongs which all writers must either meet or defeat. It is impossible, for example, to write a poem for the first time. It is, however, possible to change our understanding of what constitutes a poem, as the Romantic poets did. At a more specific level, certain texts use or quote material and techniques from previous texts, the most popular source for this being the Bible. When you write about a text's literary context you should try to situate it in its genre, showing how it does and does not live up to that genre's expectations, and demonstrate what other texts have had an influence upon it, as well as how our understanding of it has changed in the light of subsequent works.

> **Writers are influenced by other writers, and readers are influenced by other texts they have read.**

### Cultural context

The cultural context of a work of literature, in this sense at least, refers to the general artistic and philosophical movement or milieu in which it was written, as well as to the one in which it is read. For example, the present artistic movement is generally known as postmodernism. Part of the ethos of postmodernism is to question the stability of meaning and to emphasize the narrative aspects of writing history. We can identify this ethos at work in a novel like Margaret Atwood's *The Handmaid's Tale* which, with its parody of an academic symposium at the end, questions the authenticity of the tale in the rest of the text.

> **The cultural context of a work of literature refers to the general artistic and philosophical movement or milieu in which it is written and read.**

### Political context

The political context of a text refers to the point of view from which it is told and interpreted. Both New Criticism and Practical Criticism valued literature for the way in which it demonstrated the universal appeal of certain values. As most of the literature you will study has been written over the past 500 years, a period during which power has largely been in the hands of white, Western and middle-class males, it is perhaps unsurprising that their views have tended to predominate as 'universal'. In recent years, however, more attention has been paid to those that are marginalized by this point of view – which is most people. Whether you are black or white, male or female, African or European, working-class or middle-class, heterosexual or homosexual, disabled or able-bodied, any combination of these or not, it will affect what you write about, how you write it, and the values you employ when you read. When you write an essay you are not expected to assume someone else's identity, but you can maintain an awareness of the possible responses to a text. For example, the madness of Catherine in Emily Brontë's *Wuthering Heights* can be read as an individual psychological problem, or it can be read, from a feminist point of view, as the inevitable result of her loss of autonomy in a male-dominated society.

> **Your particular identity will affect what you write about, how you write it, and the values you employ when you read.**

## Historical context

The historical context of a text refers to the period in which it is written and the one in which it is read. As such, the historical context of a novel, poem or play touches upon all the other contexts I have so far discussed. Critics consider the relationship between a text and its history in several ways. First, they look at how a text embodies the values of its day. Secondly, they look at how a text helped to shape the values of its day. Thirdly, they look at the different ways in which a text has been received throughout history. You should try to develop an awareness of all of these issues about the texts you are studying. For example, Romantic poetry embodied the values of its day insofar as it focused on the growing individualism of the time. It helped to shape these values by developing the notion of the individual imagi-

> **The historical context of a text refers to the period in which it is written and the one in which it is read.**

nation. However, with the advent of modernism, Romantic poetry was seen as too individualistic and it is only in recent years that it has come back into favour.

## WRITING ABOUT CONTEXT

You are not expected, and nor will you be able, to write about all of these different aspects of context in a single essay. As the word 'context' itself suggests, writing about context is a matter of relevance. The relevance of an aspect of a text's context depends upon the particular argument of your essay. If you are writing a feminist analysis of Jane Austen's *Pride and Prejudice*, for example, the context of the Napoleonic Wars is probably not strictly pertinent to your argument. What it is important to remember, however, is that a text is inseparable from its contexts. Although your focus in an essay should be on 'the words on the page', your analysis of those words is mediated by your own context – the resonances particular words have for you, what literary influences you recognize in the text, the particular culture within which you are writing, what gender, race, creed or sexuality you are, and the history of the country and continent you are writing from. Context, in this sense, is therefore an awareness about your own critical practice, about what you write and why you write it.

> **A text is inseparable from its contexts, both when it is written and when it is read.**

### Always ask yourself:

✔ How does my reading of the text compare with other possible analyses of it, and what factors influence the differences?

✔ What comparisons can be drawn between this text and other texts?

✔ What are the historical contexts of the text, and if they are different from my own, how does that difference manifest itself?

# Analysing the structure of comedy

## 14

*Question: Why did the chicken cross the road? Answer: To get to the other side. The chances are that you've heard this joke before, but can you say what is funny about it, if indeed anything is? Furthermore, do you have to find it funny in the first place in order to be able to articulate where the humour lies in the joke or even to recognize it as a joke at all? Most students actually find it quite difficult to write about comic incidents in texts. This is because either they do not recognize something as funny in the first place or, if they do, they are not sure why it is funny, or at least meant to be funny. As many essay questions ask you to analyse the humour of a text, this chapter examines some of the theories about what makes us laugh.*

## YOU DO NOT HAVE TO FIND SOMETHING FUNNY TO FIND IT FUNNY

There is clearly something funny or odd in writing about what makes us laugh. The process of literary analysis is usually conceived as a serious business whereas comedy, by definition, is not. In addition, analysing a text requires you to stop and think about it, to turn things over in your mind, whereas laughing at a joke or comic incident is an instantaneous response which seems to by-pass the brain and go straight for the belly. Applying analysis to comedy, then, would only seem to take all the fun out of laughter. That is undoubtedly a weakness of comic analysis, but it is also a strength because it means you do not have to laugh at something to find it funny.

> **You do not have to laugh at a text in order to able to analyse its comedy.**

Let me show you what I mean. Take another look at the age-old joke about the chicken crossing the road. Why is that funny?

1   The phrase 'Why did the chicken. . .?' grants the chicken a sense of volition or intention. The joke either supposes that chickens are able to articulate good causes for doing something or that we can at least infer them from their behaviour – 'Ah, the chicken has his reasons'. However, most chickens, as far as we know, are animals who spend their time mindlessly pecking at seed. The premise of the joke, then, depends either on there being a secret world of philosophical chickens or on our understanding the chicken as we would a person, bestowing upon it the power of a mutant hybrid human-chicken.

2   This particular chicken crosses the road. Again, crossing a road belongs to the register or type of phrases associated with describing human activities. If you cross a road, as opposed to flapping your way over that black stretch of land in front of you, you are aware of what a road is, why it might be dangerous, how to avoid that danger, and so on. At some level, then, the phrase 'Why did the chicken cross the road?' conjures up an image of a hen or rooster diligently waiting on the pavement for all the cars to pass by before calmly walking across the road, all the while looking left and right in accordance with the Green Cross Code.

3   Having set up the premise of the joke, which is that there is this law-abiding and utterly reasonable chicken, the answer to the question turns out to be that all the chicken wanted to do was to get to the other side of the road. There is, in other words, no great or meaningful purpose to this chicken's unnaturally enlarged intellect. The punch-line therefore plays on two aspects of the premise. First, we have been fooled into believing the chicken wanted to do something extraordinary by crossing the road, because the premise of the joke gives it extraordinary non-chicken powers, in which case the joke is on us and our deflated expectations. Secondly, the joke is on the chicken because having assumed these philosophical gifts it wastes them by using them just to get across the road, which we take for granted by doing every day of the week.

These are three of the aspects of the joke (and there are others) which make it funny, whether you laugh at it or not. What these features have in common is a sense of incongruity or anomaly, by which I mean that the three causes of humour in the joke are all structured around a discrepancy between what we expect to happen and what does happen. So, for example, we do not expect chickens to have reasons but in the joke the chicken does have a reason. We do not expect chickens to cross roads, but in the joke one does cross a road. And we do not expect the chicken, having crossed the road and been granted the power of reason, merely to cross the road in order to get to the other side. In each case, it is the discrepancy or the incongruity which makes it funny.

## THE CONTEXT OF COMEDY

In fact, discrepancy or incongruity is the reason why most comic incidents or descriptions are funny. If we see someone walking down a street we expect them either to keep walking or to stop. We do not expect them to slip on a banana skin and fall over. That is why it is funny. It is also, of course, why people slipping on banana skins is not funny and why the chicken joke is not funny any more. We now *expect* the chicken to cross the road to get to the other side, just as we now expect someone walking

**Most humour is produced by a discrepancy between what we expect to happen and what actually happens.**

towards a banana skin to slip on it, because these are hackneyed jokes. If we expect something, it's not funny because there is no discrepancy between what happens and what we assume will happen.

If comedy depends on our expectations, where do our expectations come from? The two main sources are the *cultural context* and the *textual context*.

## Cultural context

The cultural context is the context in which we read a text. It includes the epoch we live in, the values we hold and what we expect people to do and say in specific circumstances given our own experience. For example, in the short story 'A Good Man is Hard to Find' by Flannery O'Connor, The Misfit politely asks the mother if she would like to take her daughter and join her husband and her sons in the wood, to which she replies, '"Yes, thank you"'. There is a dark humour in this, sometimes called gallows humour, because she knows that her husband and sons have just been murdered in the wood and we do not expect people to be so polite and emotionally detached either when they are about to murder someone, as in the case of The Misfit, or when they are about to be murdered, as in the case of the mother. In other words, the humour is produced by the incongruous use of manners in a situation where the characters are being so uncivilized.

## Textual context

The textual context is the context set up by the text itself. It includes the way in which characters have been represented so far and the type of register the text employs. For example, when, in Charles Dickens's *David Copperfield*, Mr Micawber prefixes a sentence by saying 'In short' or 'I will be brief' it is funny because contrary to the expectations set up by these statements, he is never short or brief in what he says. In other words, there is a discrepancy between Micawber's intentions and what he actually does.

## COMMON TYPES OF COMEDY

There are many different types of comedy in literature. Wherever possible you should try and use the correct technical term to describe them. To help you here are some of the more common figures of speech which produce a comic effect:

- **Catachresis** A catachresis is the incorrect use of a word. For example, 'Aunt Nelly told them the funeral courgette was here'. Obviously, Nelly meant to say 'cortège' instead of 'courgette'. A catachresis also refers to a mixed metaphor, such as 'Dom flew in the face of the opposing tide until, finally, he had run his legs off'. Clearly here the metaphorical descriptions of Dom's actions are incongruous with each other as you cannot fly through water while running at the same time.
- **Hyperbole** A hyperbole is a form of exaggeration. For example, 'Sophie thought of a million reasons why she should not go in before she entered her father's study'. This is an exaggeration because if Sophie had literally thought of a million reasons she probably would have died of old age before she entered the study.
- **Irony** Irony is a way of saying one thing while meaning another. It relies for its effect on the context in which it is made. For example, when Jonathan Swift's 'A

Modest Proposal' suggests selling and eating babies as a way of alleviating Ireland's famine, it is ironic because it is obviously not acceptable to eat babies in our culture.

* **Litotes** A litotes is a form of understatement. For example, 'Emma was not a little grieved at Mr Elton's reaction' is a negative expression of the fact that Emma is in fact very grieved at Mr Elton's reaction.
* **Paronomasia** A paronomasia is a pun or play on words. For example, 'The nun said she was not in the habit of wearing such clothes' is a pun upon the word 'habit' which can mean both a routine and a type of dress that nuns wear.
* **Zeugma** A zeugma is where one word is used to modify the meaning of two unrelated or incongruous words or phrases. For example, in the sentence 'Mr Pickwick took his hat and his leave', the verb 'to take' refers both to Pickwick's hat and his leaving.

**Always ask yourself:**
* ✔ What is the discrepancy which produces the humour?
* ✔ What type of context produces the expectation which is thwarted by the comedy?
* ✔ Am I using the correct technical term to describe the comic effect I am writing about?

## 15

# Analysing the reader's response

*If you are asked what your response is to a book, the chances are that you will say either that you like it or that you don't. This response is normally perfectly adequate – unless, of course, the question is posed in an exam paper. As you will no doubt already know, many exam questions are phrased around your response to a particular text or extract. And as you are also probably aware, these questions are difficult to answer. This is because your response is likely to be a combination of thoughts and feelings, some of which are hard to articulate in language. On top of this, you may well suppose you are being asked to create a response that matches those of the exam board, rather than offering your own. This chapter is designed to help you overcome these diffi-culties by outlining some of the theories which, in recent years, have been used to explain how texts and readers interact to produce a response.*

## LITERARY COMPETENCE

What actually happens when you read a novel, or a poem, or a play? The answer is 'a lot'. It may not seem like it, but reading is hard work. The reason it may not seem like it is because most of the labour of reading goes on unnoticed. Let me show you what I mean by looking at the first line of James Joyce's 'The Sisters' – 'There was no hope for him this time: it was the third stroke.' What does this mean? Consider a few of the possibilities:

- To whom does the 'him' refer? It could be a large guppy fish, or it could be a baby dragon. It could refer to one of the sisters of the title in the final stages of a trans-gender operation. Given that this is a story by Joyce, however, who rarely ever wrote about guppy fish, dragons or trans-gender operations, we assume that 'him' refers to a male human being.
- What is the 'third stroke'? Is it the stroke of a clock, the stroke of a whip, the stroke of genius, the stroke of an oar or the third stroke at the ball in a game of baseball? Perhaps that is why this mysterious figure has no hope – it was his third attempt to hit the ball and now he's out. But as this story comes from a book about turn-of-the-century Dublin, such an interpretation is unlikely.
- Maybe the stroke has nothing to do with the man or boy in question and it actu-ally refers to a magic self-propelling axe in Guatemala hacking at a miniature trombone. Again, this is improbable, first because it is a linguistic convention that that the two sides of a sentence separated by a colon relate to each other, and, secondly, because *Dubliners* (from which the story is taken) belongs to the genre of realism.

Most of you will have safely assumed that this sentence describes a man about to die from the rupture of a blood vessel in the brain. You will not consciously have gone through all these different permutations to reach this conclusion. Instead you will have filtered out the other possible interpretations of the opening sentence either before you read it or while you were reading it. You probably don't remember doing it, so how did you do it?

The short answer is that you employed your *literary competence*. Literary competence is the set of conventions which influence the way we interpret and respond to literature. This book is largely an explanation of some of these conventions, but there are many more which you will already know. For example, you already know that speech is conventionally represented in novels by quotation marks. When a novel uses quotation marks, then, it expects you, as a reader, to know that they signify speech. The novel expects, in other words, that its reader will have a certain degree of literary competence.

> **Literary competence is the set of conventions which influence the way we interpret and respond to literature.**

Literary competence is made up of three main components:

1  **The reality convention** The reality convention makes sense of a text in terms of the real world. For example, when Amelia Sedley starts crying in William Thackeray's *Vanity Fair*, we assume that she doesn't continue to cry for ever because in real life most people do not weep for the whole of their lives.

2  **The cultural convention** The cultural convention makes sense of a text in terms of the generally accepted conventions of a culture. For example, when Oedipus pokes his own eyes out in Sophocles's *Oedipus Rex*, we accept this as an understandable reaction (for someone who has just found out that he has killed his father and spawned several children with his mother) because in our culture patricide and incest are abominable crimes.

3  **The generic convention** The generic convention makes sense of a text in terms of the expectations we have about a genre. For example, we are not surprised to see half a dozen corpses on the stage at the end of Shakespeare's *King Lear* because we watch it as a tragedy. If we watched it in terms of the genre of comedy, however, we might expect all the corpses to get up again and do a little jig.

When you analyse your response to a text, you need to examine the ways in which the text corresponds or not to the expectations of these different conventions. For example, one of the most challenging scenes in contemporary literature is Cholly's rape of his daughter Pecola in Toni Morrison's *The Bluest Eye*. Part of the difficulty of the scene lies in the way Cholly's actions are described in terms of 'tenderness' and 'protectiveness'. As Morrison herself comments, 'I want you to look at him and see his love for his daughter and his powerlessness to help her pain. By that time his embrace, his rape, is all the gift he has left.' Our response to this scene, then, would normally be one of shocked abhorrence, but that response is confused by the pathos we feel for Cholly.

## READERLY AND WRITERLY TEXTS

Every time you read a text your literary competence is confirmed or confronted. If you see a tragedy in which all the dead

> **When you analyse your response to a text, you need to examine the ways in which the text corresponds or not to your expectations about reality, culture and genre.**

people stay dead and the characters that start crying finish crying a short while later, and so on, all your expectations will have been met. If, on the other hand, you see a tragedy in which all the characters laugh hysterically all the way through, attempting to kill each other with custard pies, your expectations will not have been met.

> **A readerly text is one that conforms to our expectations; a writerly text is one that confronts our expectations.**

This will then unsettle your notion of what a tragedy is and you may subsequently revise your expectations. The French critic Roland Barthes divides texts up between those that conform to expectations – *readerly texts* – and those that confront

them – *writerly texts*. He argues that each type of text produces a different type of response.

- **Readerly texts** A readerly text is one that conforms to expectations. It is comfortable to read and merely affirms all your stereotypes of reality, culture and genre. It is called a readerly text because you just passively read it. This type of text produces in its reader a feeling of contentment or what Barthes terms 'pleasure'.
- **Writerly texts** A writerly text is one that confronts your expectations. It is unsettling to read and may change the way you think about conceptions of reality, culture or genre. It is called a writerly text because to read it compels you to think actively about it. This type of text produces in its reader a feeling of estrangement or what Barthes terms 'rapture'.

The difference between readerly and writerly texts is a matter of degree, like the difference between eating a chocolate bar and paragliding off Mount Everest. Both are enjoyable experiences, but while one is merely nice, the other is stunning.

You will have noticed that I have not given any examples of each type of text. This is because whether you consider a specific text to be pleasurable or rapturous depends both on your literary competence and on how you approach it in the first place. If, for example, you had read Wordsworth's early poems at the time they were first published, you might have considered them to be writerly texts. This is because Wordsworth's use of common, or quotidian, diction was highly unusual at the time and would have unsettled your idea of what type of language should make up a poem. As an early twenty-first-century reader, however, you might think of Wordsworth's poems as readerly texts precisely because they have become the dominant conception of what poetry should look and sound like.

> **Whether you consider a text to be readerly or writerly depends both on the make-up of your literary competence and how you approach the text.**

In a sense, of course, all texts are writerly if you actively think about them enough – that is, if you analyse them. There is usually something strange and unsettling about every poem, novel and play. Part of your job when writing essays is to look for those writerly moments. So, for example, you might expect poems to look like Wordsworth's poems, but when you think about it, isn't there something discomforting about poetry in the first place, the way the language is compacted and given rhythm? If you think so, then you have discovered a writerly moment in the text, something that estranges your notion of the use of language.

## SUSPENSE

One of the main ways in which a text prompts a response from its reader is by generating suspense. There are two basic categories of suspense – *resolved* and *unresolved*.

- **Resolved suspense** Suspense is resolved when the reader knows what happens or is left certain of the outcome. There are two types of resolved suspense. The first type proceeds from effect to cause and involves the text withholding the answer to a question. For example, in Arthur Miller's *The Crucible* suspense is generated by us not knowing what will happen to the women accused of witchcraft. The second type of resolved suspense proceeds from cause to effect and involves the text delaying the completion of an action we expect to happen. For example, when at the end of Act One of Henrik Ibsen's *Hedda Gabler*, Hedda brings out her father's pistols, we expect that some time later in the play someone will get shot. This suspense is resolved when Hedda shoots herself at the end of Act Four.
- **Unresolved suspense** Suspense remains unresolved when the reader is left in doubt about what actually happened or uncertain of the meaning of a text. For example, Henry James's *The Turn of the Screw* ends ambiguously because the reader is not certain whether the governess is hallucinating or actually sees ghosts.

The difference between the two types of suspense lies in the reader's response to them. With resolved suspense the reader takes an immediate interest in the text by wanting to find out what will happen next. A reader's response to texts of this kind is likely to be anxiety and tension. With unresolved suspense the reader takes a delayed interest in the text, going back through it in order to try and resolve its ambiguity. A reader's response to texts of this kind is likely to be puzzled and pensive. In this sense, the difference

> **Resolved suspense is how the text keeps itself alive while you are reading it; unresolved suspense is how the text keeps itself alive after you have read it.**

between the two types of suspense is also largely a matter of whether a text is readerly or writerly – that is, whether you are passively hooked by a text, in the case of resolved suspense, or actively think about it, in the case of unresolved suspense.

## WRITING ABOUT YOUR RESPONSE

The response you have to a text is as individual as you are. What I have tried to do here is provide a framework of issues through which you can express your response. The basic rule of writing about your response is to ground it in the text. Explain how the text attempts to coerce a

> **The basic rule of writing about your response is to relate it to the text.**

response from you and explain what factors influence your response.

Take a look at the following extract from an essay on Anton Chekov's *The Cherry Orchard*:

*The Cherry Orchard* is a strange play because it is neither a tragedy or a comedy. It begins with a marriage that doesn't quite happen and ends with a death that doesn't quite happen, so in the end nothing really happens. Nor do the characters develop. They just move in and out of the play like the train they arrive and depart on. This is quite frustrating because you want the characters to stop flitting about and actually do something. I kept waiting for something dramatic but the play ends as unresolved as the fate of Russia precisely because the characters do not do anything.

This is quite a good example of the way in which you should write about your response to a text because:

1   It contextualizes the student's response in terms of her expectations of the genres of comedy and tragedy.
2   Even though the student's response to the play is not completely positive, the essay locates and explains the source of her feelings of 'strangeness' and 'frustration' in the play.
3   The essay relates the student's response to the themes of the play, in this case the unresolved fate of Russia.

**Always ask yourself:**
✔   Is my response to the text based on the fact that it confirms or confronts my expectations about reality, culture or genre?
✔   What features of the text try to coerce a response from me?
✔   How does my response relate to the themes of the text?

# SECTION 3

# Genre

# Analysing different types of drama

## 16

The word 'drama' derives from the Greek verb 'to do'. Essentially it refers to the performance of an action. For this performance to happen requires three basic components – someone to perform (the actors), something to perform (the play itself) and someone to watch the performance (the audience). This chapter concentrates on the second of these components, the play itself. It is important that when you write about an individual play you also maintain an awareness of the genre from which it comes and how that genre is manifest in the individual drama. This chapter will therefore examine some of the main types of drama and look at the ways in which dramatic form has changed over the centuries.

## A BRIEF HISTORY OF DRAMA

The history of drama may broadly be thought of as the slow collapse of the hierarchies upon which it was originally based. These hierarchies involved two considerations – the subject matter of the plays and the position of drama within society. They impacted upon each other to greater or lesser degrees down the course of the centuries, but, at least initially, the position or standing of drama within society was of more importance to the subject matter of the play itself rather than vice versa.

The earliest recorded plays, such as *Antigone* and *Oedipus the King*, were performed during state-sponsored festivals, most notably the *Lenaea* and the *Dionysia*. These plays upheld the transcendental authority of the Greek gods, upon which also rested the authority of the state. With the advent of Christianity in the Roman Empire, acting was outlawed and drama almost disappeared from Europe altogether. Gradually, though, during the Middle Ages, drama was resurrected by and within the church. This resurrection initially took the form of Mystery plays which were short dramatizations of scenes from the Bible performed by priests and their attendants in Latin. The Mystery plays were themselves only an extension of the theatrical nature of church-going at the time in which crowds would go from church to church to watch Mass. Over time, the Mystery plays were translated into the vernacular and performed by the various trade guilds as part of town festivals. In addition, Miracle and Morality plays were developed which, despite being religious in theme, were more secular in that they dealt with non-biblical stories.

The process of secularization continued with the Reformation, which was a movement to reform the Catholic church,

> **The earliest plays were state-sponsored and upheld the authority of the gods.**

> **Most plays during the Middle Ages were either performed by the church or had religious subject matter.**

partly involving the removal of theatrical elements from it. This created the conditions for the building of the first fully secular theatre in Britain in the late sixteenth century. It did not, however, allow dramatists *carte blanche* to write about whatever they liked as there was still strict political censorship. So if playwrights like Shakespeare no longer had to pay direct homage to the church, they did have to pay homage to the monarch of the day who was then next in line to God. Plays such as *Richard II* or *Henry IV* are therefore concerned with themes like reinforcing the divine rights of kings to rule and establishing the rights of succession.

The problems of who should succeed Elizabeth I and which church – Catholic or Protestant – was the true one became

> **The first fully secular theatre was not built in Britain until the sixteenth century.**

manifest in the bloody intrigues of Jacobean drama in which all hierarchies seem to collapse. Following this most theatre was again banned in Britain until these sensitive political and religious issues were finally settled. The type of drama that emerged following the Restoration was rarely concerned with gods or kings any more. Instead the new focus became the competing claims of the aristocracy and the rising merchant classes of the time – a conflict which was often dramatized as a battle over matters of taste, manners and decorum, or basically money versus class. The theatre itself, although still subject to state censorship, no longer formed part of the state and was gradually becoming a diversion for the middle classes.

> **In the latter half of the seventeenth and eighteenth centuries plays were less about gods and monarchs and more about money and class.**

The gentrification of drama was completed by the advent of realism in the theatre in the works of playwrights such as Henrik Ibsen and Anton Chekov. The plays of these dramatists were largely concerned with the problems of middle-class life, problems which centred upon the reorganization of traditional hierarchies such as those between men and women. Although these problems would form the subject matter for much theatre over the next hundred years, theatre also turned in on itself and began to look at its increasingly marginal status in society. This manifested itself in plays about plays, such as in the work of Luigi Pirandello, in attempts to repoliticize the theatre, such as in the work of Bertolt Brecht, and in attempts to broaden the subject matter of theatre, such as in the work of John Osborne. However, by the end of the twentieth century theatre-going had become a marginal activity, its lack of power having been confirmed by the removal of all censorship in Britain in 1968.

> **By the end of the nineteenth century the theatre was more concerned with middle-class life.**

## TYPES OF DRAMA

The story of drama, then, traces its movement from being a state-sponsored activity with strictly defined themes to being a marginal activity with the freedom to explore any issue it wishes. Within this general picture of the dramatic genre it is possible to identify a number of different types of drama. As Greek tragedy, Renaissance drama, Restoration comedy and Epic Theatre are explored in the following chapters, I will omit them from the following discussion.

> State censorship of the theatre only ended in Britain in 1968 – a fact celebrated by a naked performance of the play *Hair* the following day.

### Jacobean tragedy

'Jacobean' refers to the reign (1603–1625) of James I of England and Ireland or James VI in Scotland ('they' were the same person). Dramatists writing during this time include William Shakespeare, Thomas Kyd, John Webster, Thomas Middleton and Philip Massinger. The Jacobean era is chiefly known for its tragedies, often called revenge tragedies. These plays differ from other types of tragedy because the tragic hero is replaced by a collective of what had previously been the minor characters of the court. These characters do not exhibit heroic courage either but cunning, conniving amidst numerous, obscure plots which invariably result in the hideous and bizarre deaths of almost everyone on stage.

### Realism

Realism is the kind of drama with which we are most familiar, not least because it is the dominant form of film and television. Its main purpose is to imitate life more closely than other types of drama. To this end it tends to use prose dialogue rather than verse, employs convincing scenery, and concentrates upon 'ordinary' topics rather than heroes, myths and monarchies. The works of Henrik Ibsen, Anton Chekov and Arthur Miller are realist. Of course, realism is not completely 'realistic'. For example, many realist plays employ symbolism of one type or another, turning the sound of a broken guitar string in *The Cherry Orchard*, for instance, into a symbol for discord.

### Expressionism

If realism tries to depict the world as it really is, expressionism attempts to portray the world as we experience it. In this sense it is a subjective rather than an objective form of theatre in the same way that Van Gogh's paintings are a subjective form of painting. The works of August Strindberg, Elmer Rice and Tennessee Williams are predominantly expressionist. Expressionist theatre tends to rely quite heavily on stage effects in order to convey the emotive expression of its characters. For example, to connote the fact that Williams's play *The Glass Menagerie* is the expression of Tom's memory, the stage directions urge the director to use lighting to pick out particular objects and transmit a mood, to use a certain type of soundtrack because 'memory always happens to music' and to project phrases on a backdrop to highlight the underlying process of the characters' thoughts.

### The theatre of the absurd

This term relates to the work of playwrights such as Samuel Beckett, Eugène Ionesco and Harold Pinter. The 'absurdity' refers to both the themes and the forms of these dramas. In terms of themes, these writers were influenced by the school of philosophy known as existentialism which argues that, because God is either dead or completely absent, life has no intrinsic meaning. In order to reflect this absurd predicament, plays of this kind tend to dispense with any sense of conventional plot (because there is no order to the world), with characterization (because we all lack identity and are alienated) and with dialogue (because we are all isolated from one another).

As with all descriptions of genres, these definitions are by no means watertight. For example, from the point of view of an existentialist, the theatre of the absurd is highly realistic, whereas for someone who believes in God such theatre will appear highly idiosyncratic and therefore a mode of expressionism. Equally, Shakespeare's *Hamlet* shares some of the qualities of a Jacobean or revenge tragedy, based as it is on a court intrigue which ends in the massacre of most of its principal characters, yet because it has in Hamlet a tragic hero it does not quite fall into that category. What these definitions do is provide a context or framework of reference within which to understand the play you are studying. They allow you to connect different plays with each other and thereby increase the depth of your analysis.

> **The same play can have elements of different genres within it.**

### Always ask yourself:

✔   What is the context of this play and how does that context affect it?

✔   What type of drama is this play?

✔   How does it differ from other plays which belong to this type of drama and what effect does this difference have?

## 17

# Analysing tragic drama

*A tragedy in life is commonly defined as a great misfortune or a shocking and sad event. This definition has much in common with the definition of tragic drama. In particular, tragic drama is also defined by a story which involves a descent into calamity and by the production of an overwhelming or shocking emotion as a result of this misfortune. It is a definition as familiar to us as it was to Chaucer: 'Tragedie is to seyn a certeyn storie . . . / Of hym that stood in greet prosperitee / And is yfallen out of heigh degree / Into myserie, and endeth wrecchedly'. The reason that, for both Chaucer and us, tragedy involves the wretched end of someone who formerly stood in great prosperity is that the framework or ground rules for tragic drama were set down in fourth-century BC Greece.*

## ARISTOTLE'S *POETICS*

The man who laid these ground rules was called Aristotle. Aristotle was a Greek philosopher whose thinking influenced much of the world on everything from logic and ethics to zoology and poetics. Poetics is the study of the principles of literature. The surviving fragments of Aristotle's book on the subject (you may remember that the rest of it was burnt at the end of Umberto Eco's *The Name of the Rose*) form the basis for our understanding of tragedy.

> **Aristotle's *Poetics* still forms the basis for our understanding of tragedy.**

Aristotle developed his analysis of tragedy on the great Greek dramas of the time which, in essence, were composed of the following features:

- **The protagonist** The protagonist, which derives from the Greek words for 'first actor', is the principal or leading character in a play. Othello, for example, is the protagonist of Shakespeare's *Othello*. Hamlet is the protagonist of Shakespeare's *Hamlet*.
- **The antagonist** The antagonist, which derives from the Greek word for 'strive' or 'contest', is the principal opponent or adversary of the protagonist. Iago, for example, is the antagonist of *Othello* because of the way he tries to undermine the play's protagonist, Othello. Similarly, Claudius is the chief antagonist of *Hamlet*.
- **Hamartia** Hamartia, which derives from the Greek word for 'error', refers to the mistaken judgement of the protagonist. Hamartia is sometimes translated as

'tragic flaw', which intimates that the protagonist's error of judgement is in-built or part of the character's make-up. Othello's hamartia is that he believes Iago about Desdemona's handkerchief. Hamlet's hamartia is that he postpones his decision to confront Claudius.

- **Hubris** Hubris, which derives from the Greek word for 'pride', is a particular form of hamartia, one which denotes in the protagonist an arrogance or over-confident belief in his or her abilities. The classic image of hubris can be found in the myth of Icarus. Despite being cautioned by his father, Icarus constructed wings out of wax and feathers, and when he flew too near the sun the wax melted and he fell into the sea. Excessive ambition like this can also be found in Christopher Marlowe's *Doctor Faustus*, whose protagonist thinks he can bargain with the Devil for everything he wants and still not have to pay the consequences with his soul.

- **Peripeteia** Peripeteia, which derives from the Greek verb 'to fall' or 'to change suddenly', refers to a reversal in fortune or an abrupt change in events for the protagonist of a tragedy. For example, Othello's fortunes change when Iago begins to plot against him. However, as tragedies very often contain an element of fatedness or predestination, it is not always clear where the peripeteia takes place. For example, Macbeth's downfall is foretold by the three witches very near the beginning of the play but Birnan wood is not moved to Dunsinane and Macbeth is not actually killed by Macduff till near the end. Similarly, Oedipus's downfall, in Sophocles's *Oedipus the King*, is predicted by the Oracle before he is even born, so it is not clear whether he can have a reversal of fortune when his fortune is already predetermined.

- **Anagnorisis** Anagnorisis, which comes from the Greek word for 'recognition', designates moment of self-awareness when the protagonist realizes that he or she is in some way doomed. It tends to be a more useful concept than peripeteia because it can be identified quite precisely in the text. For example, Macbeth's anag-norisis – 'Accursèd be that tongue that tells me so; / For it hath cowed my better part of man' – comes when Macduff tells him that he was born by Caesarean section, thus confirming the prophecy of the witches that he would be killed by a man not born of woman. Similarly, although Oedipus has been doomed since birth, he only realizes it towards the end of the play – 'I, Oedipus . . . / damned in his birth, in his marriage damned, / damned in the blood he shed with his own hand.'

These elements can be found more or less in every classic tragedy. They combine to form a story in which the protagonist begins the play either already at the height of his or her fortune or about to reach it. However, the very character trait which helped him or her to ascend to the zenith of his or her powers turns out to be the tragic flaw or hamartia which, when exercised to its full, proves to be the protago-nist's undoing. The downfall of the protagonist then proceeds apace, often helped by the antagonist, and also often unknown to the protagonist until the moment of anagnorisis or self-awareness when the hero or heroine realizes that they are doomed because of what they have done.

If that is the story of a tragedy, Aristotle also argued that this story should be accompanied by, and should produce in its audience, specific emotions. To this end, he proposed that tragic drama should be composed of 'incidents arous-

> **Tragedies are basically the stories of the downfall of heroes caused by tragic flaws in their characters.**

ing pity and fear, in order to accomplish its catharsis of such emotions'.

- **Catharsis** Catharsis, which derives from the Greek word for 'purge', refers to the release or purifying of emotions at the end of a tragedy. For Aristotle the particular emotions which are purged by the feeling of catharsis following the climax of a play are pity and fear. These emotions are inspired by the tragic downfall of the play's protagonist – we feel pity at their wretched state at the same time as we feel fear at what happens to them. So, for example, we are horrified by Gloucester (in Shakespeare's *King Lear*) having his eyes put out and we also pity him for that fate.

## BERTOLT BRECHT'S REVISION OF ARISTOTLE

Since Aristotle conceived his *Poetics* almost every major writer and philosopher has had something to say about his theory. One of the most influential rewritings of Aristotle's theory is by the German playwright Bertolt Brecht. Brecht's basic argument is that at the beginning of a tragedy the audience empathizes with the protagonist, including with his or her hamartia. Crucially for Brecht, the hero's hamartia almost always involves some kind of social hubris – which is to say the tragic flaw of the protagonist is some characteristic which contravenes the social order. For example, Macbeth's hamartia is his desire to usurp the king and become king himself. In other words, he does not know his place. During the play the audience's identification with the protagonist continues until the point of peripeteia and anagnorisis. When the tragic hero suffers a reversal of fortune and a terrible and usually terminal fate, the audience stops identifying with him or her. In this way, the audience's catharsis is really a purging of their identification with the hero's tragic flaw – the anti-social characteristic.

> **For Bertolt Brecht a character's tragic flaw is a form of social hubris which means the hero does not know his or her place in life.**

For Brecht, then, tragic drama is a form of social coercion designed to keep people in their place. Indeed, he thought that most drama, including film, is a way of enforcing the status quo. If this sounds far fetched, think of an ordinary television programme like *Casualty*. In a standard episode the audience are introduced to several characters with whom they can identify because of their very ordinariness. We then find out that these characters have all committed some kind of social crime – like having an affair, chopping down their neighbour's tree without permission, or playing truant. As a result of this social deviancy the characters are then subject to horrific accidents of one kind or another in which they either die or suffer terribly. It is at this point that the audience stops identifying with the characters and we are purged of our desire to chop down our neighbours' trees without permission in case we too fall off a ladder and a chainsaw lands on top of us.

## WRITING ABOUT TRAGIC DRAMA

If, when you are writing your essay, you can apply the technical names to each part of a tragedy and show an appreciation of its trajectory in terms of Aristotle's theory then you will demonstrate a solid under-

> **When you write about tragedy, try to use the correct technical terms if you can.**

standing of the most influential analysis of theatre ever written and increase your chances of getting a higher grade. Let me show you what I mean. This is an extract taken from an essay on the topic 'Examine and explain the development of the character of Oedipus in Sophocles's *Oedipus the King*'.

One interesting thing about the development of Oedipus's character during the play is how the audience's reaction to his character changes. By leaving what he thought was his parents in case he should harm them, as the Oracle predicted, he performs an action with which the audience can empathize. However, by the end of the play we do not empathize with Oedipus at all, even though we pity him. This is because he showed hubris in trying to avoid the fate the gods had set for him and he ends up being blinded. It is also possible that as we do not believe in the Greek gods any more we would neither empathize with his initial decision nor feel fear at his downfall, as Aristotle hoped, because we do not feel his fate could ever be ours.

Despite sitting on the fence a little, this is a good essay because, first, it employs the correct technical terms at appropriate moments, for example 'pity', 'fear' and 'hubris'. Secondly, the essay also recognizes the difference between Sophocles's Greek audience and one from our own day. In other words, the essay writer contextualizes his or her own response to the play in terms of Aristotle's theory. This is a valid tactic because it shows the writer has considered his or her reaction in the light of accepted theory.

> **Even if your response to a tragedy is not the same as Aristotle's, it is a good idea to show how your response differs from his.**

**Always ask yourself:**
- ✔ Does this play follow Aristotle's blueprint for the development of a tragedy?
- ✔ What is my reaction to the tragedy and how does it compare to Aristotle's *Poetics*?
- ✔ Am I using the correct technical terms to describe the characters and events in the play?

# Analysing comic drama

## 18

*If tragedy is about the downfall of an individual, it is often said that comedy is about the downfall of society as a whole. This does not mean that everybody on stage dies in some sort of apocalypse; rather it refers to the predominant theme in comic drama which is the social bond. Comedies tend to be about the way in which society is organized, the rules and ethos that hold society together, and, in particular, the way in which the ideal embodiment of a society is never matched by a really existing society. These themes have been taken up and dramatized in different ways by playwrights across the centuries, and this chapter will look at some of the more important types of comic drama.*

## HIGH AND LOW COMEDY

One way of distinguishing between types of comedy is to employ the categories first put forward by the nineteenth-century critic George Meredith. Meredith argues that there are basically two types of comedy – high and low.

- **Low comedy** Low comedy is basically slapstick, physical comedy and vulgar or ribald humour of the type associated with bodily activities. It is unlikely that you will ever study a play that is entirely made up of low comedy, but many plays use moments of low comedy either as a weapon in their comic arsenal or as a form of comic relief. For example, when Bottom's head is turned into the head of an ass in Shakespeare's *A Midsummer Night's Dream* this is a moment of low comedy.
- **High comedy** High comedy is comedy that appeals to the intellect and is therefore more likely to be made up of witticisms, puns, aphorisms and verbal ripostes. The work of Oscar Wilde is an example of high comedy. You are more likely to study this kind of comedy as it tends to be the predominant form of comic drama, as well as lending itself better to the written word than low comedy.

## TYPES OF COMEDY

In terms of high comedy, there are two main types of comic drama you are most likely to study – comedy of humours and Restoration comedy, or comedy of manners.

### Comedy of humours

A comedy of humours refers to a play that draws for its characters upon stock types who are based around dominant character traits or humours. According to medieval medical theory, the body was chiefly constituted by four liquids – blood, phlegm, choler (or yellow bile) and melancholy (or black bile). If these liquids, or humours, were kept in balance a person was thought to be in good health or humour. However, an excess of any particular humour would lead to a person becoming sanguine, phlegmatic, choleric or melancholic. A comedy of humours simply refers to a play in which the characters are dominated by particular humours. Influenced in part by the Italian *commedia dell'arte*, which was a form of improvised theatre based on stock characters, humour comedies were popular in the sixteenth and seventeenth centuries. The most notable exponent of this type of drama is Ben Jonson, with plays like *Every Man in His Humour*, *The Alchemist* and *Bartholomew Fair*. Jonson notes of his characters in *Every Man in His Humour* that 'Some one peculiar quality / doth so possess a man, that it doth draw / All his affects, his spirits, and his powers, / In their confluctions, all to run one way.' To indicate this 'one peculiar quality' Jonson often uses highly suggestive names for his characters such as Epicure Mammon, Subtle and Zeal-of-the-land Busy. The source of the comedy

> **A comedy of humours is a play in which the characters are dominated by particular humours or characteristics.**

in these plays comes from the discrepancy between the way the characters see a situation, blinkered as they are by the exaggerated qualities of their predominant humours, and the way the situation actually is, which is usually some kind of trap or lure. For example, when, in Ben Jonson's *Volpone*, Corvino goes to visit Volpone he presumes him to be on his deathbed and that he will inherit Volpone's wealth. Blinded by his greed for the inheritance, Corvino does not think twice about leaving a diamond in Volpone's hand – as Volpone's servant reminds him 'Is not all here yours?' Of course, Volpone is only pretending to be near death and so he dupes Corvino out of the diamond.

> **The comedy in humour plays tends to come from the difference between the way a character sees the world and the way the world really is.**

### Restoration comedy and comedy of manners

Restoration comedy, or comedy of manners as it is also known, refers to the comedies written and performed following the restoration of the monarchy in 1660. Although he was shorn of effective political power, the return of Charles II from Europe marked an increase in the influence of the court on what we would now call 'high society'. The growing merchant class looked to the aristocracy to provide it with the kind of style and etiquette it felt its newfound riches deserved. Restoration comedy plays upon these themes, satirizing matters of taste and manners and the effect upon them of money. As women were now allowed to act on stage for the first time, these plays also show an increased interest in dramatizing sexual relations. Restoration comedy, in the works of playwrights such as William Wycherley and William Congreve, therefore tends to be based on wit and other kinds of verbal jousting. The humour in comedies of this type comes from the discrepancy between the accepted definitions of social institutions, such as marriage, and the way in which the characters treat those institutions. For example, in Congreve's *The Way of the World* Mirabell and Millament forsake the romantic ideal of marriage (which was a popular theme in the tragedies of the time) for what we would now think of as a pre-nuptial agreement. Arguing that

> **Restoration comedies are dramas based on wit and verbal exchanges.**

their future life together should actually be a life apart, Millament proposes that she and Mirabell should be 'as strange as if we had been married a great while; and as well bred as if we were not married at all'. The intimacy which was generally held

> **The humour in Restoration comedies comes from the discrepancy between the accepted definitions of social institutions, such as marriage, and the way in which the characters treat those institutions.**

to be an agreeable effect of the ideal marriage is here counted as one of its drawbacks, reflecting the fact that seventeenth-century couples did not actually spend a lot of time together.

Although comedy of humours and Restoration comedy are based in specific periods of history, their genres have influenced comedy since then. Many plays, for example, have relied upon the stock types used in Jonson's dramas, and although Restoration comedy was finished as a historically specific form of drama early in the 1700s (giving way to the comedy of sentiment, such as the work of Richard Steele – a form of mawkish comedy in which the ideals of love are upheld), the tradition of satirizing manners continued later in the eighteenth century in the works of playwrights such as Oliver Goldsmith and Richard Sheridan, and even in the nineteenth century in the works of Oscar Wilde.

## WRITING ABOUT COMEDY

When you analyse a play for its humour, your primary task is to explain why something is funny, or at least explain why it is meant to be funny. It is never enough just to describe a text as funny and to quote a couple of examples and leave it at that. In order to get the highest possible grade you also need to dissect these examples and show how they achieve their comic effect. Your explanation will almost invariably centre upon the way in which humour is produced by an incongruity or an anomaly.

> **In order to get the highest possible grade you need to show how a play achieves its comic effect.**

Let me show you what I mean. Take a look at this extract from an essay which answers the question 'What comic techniques are employed in Oscar Wilde's *The Importance of Being Earnest*'?

 *The Importance of Being Earnest* is in many ways a social comedy. It draws on the tradition of the comedy of manners in its satire of a society that maintains a desperate civility at all costs. Like comedy of manners, much of the source of the humour comes from the way in which the characters in the play deal with all situations in the same courteous fashion, extending a concern for etiquette to areas of life that seem wholly inappropriate topics for it. For example, when Lady Bracknell finds out that Jack was discovered in a handbag she comments that 'to be born, or at any rate bred in a handbag, whether it had handles or not, seems to me to display a contempt for the ordinary decencies of family life that remind one of the worst excesses of the French Revolution'. Lady Bracknell here treats the French Revolution as if it were a lapse in manners, equating Jack's discovery in a handbag with the revolution's bloody atrocities. The discrepancy between the two, and their supposed effect on family life, is enormous and the comparison's absurdity can only make you laugh because you cannot take it seriously.

This is a good answer to the question for a number of reasons. First, the essay situates the play within the context of its genre, in this case the comedy of manners, and details what element of the genre it draws upon in particular, using where possible the correct technical term, which here is 'satire'. Secondly, the essay describes the way in which the play creates a humorous effect. Thirdly, it provides an example of this humorous effect and, fourthly, it analyses this specific example, explaining how it works and relating it to the comic technique of the play as a whole.

> **A good analysis of a comedy will contextualize that play within its appropriate genre.**

**Always ask yourself:**
- ✔ What genre of comic drama does the play belong to and how does this genre show itself in the play?
- ✔ Does the play utilize any moments of low comedy?
- ✔ What techniques are used to create a comic effect and how do these techniques work?

Anton Chekov once noted, 'I can hardly form an estimate of a play just by reading it'. He is not alone. A play does have an existence on the page but it is incomplete. This is because a play is not meant to be read; it is meant to be performed. Examiners' reports habitually lament the fact that students do not consider or discuss the performance aspect of plays. In order to help rectify this problem and so help you get a better grade, this chapter will look at the factors which you have to take into account when considering the staging and performance of a play.

## OFF THE PAGE AND ON TO THE STAGE

When you read a play on the page it is best to think of it as a script rather than a complete text in itself. This script is only one aspect of a play, albeit the most important. Between the page and the stage a play can and will change enormously. This difference is largely down to the work of the director, who will create his or her own version or production of the play. In order to understand quite how big a difference a director makes to a play you should try and see as many versions of the plays you are studying as possible. The differences between these productions will centre upon the four main issues which directors have to consider when they put on a play – the type of play, the setting, the *mise en scène* and the acting.

> **The difference between a play on the page and a play on the stage is the difference between an author and a director.**

## Type of play

The first question you need to ask about a play in terms of its performance is, what type of drama is it? If at one end of the spectrum you have tragedies and at the other end you have comedies, where does the play you are studying fall on this continuum? This question relates not to the actual script of the play but to the way it is performed. Although this is less of an issue for more clear-cut examples of each genre, such as Shakespeare's *King Lear* or *Othello*, it is a more pressing problem for

> **A director has to decide whether a play is to be produced as a tragedy, a comedy or a hybrid of the two.**

directors of tragi-comic plays such as Shakespeare's *The Tempest*, Anton Chekov's *The Cherry Orchard* or Samuel Beckett's *Waiting for Godot*.

Chekov's *The Cherry Orchard* is an interesting example of this problem.

Constantin Stanislavsky, the first director of the play, considered it to be a tragedy, whereas Chekov himself thought it was a comedy. The result of Stanislavsky's reading of the play culminated in Chekov's famous complaint against the director's production that Act 4, which he thought should have lasted 12 minutes, actually lasted 40 minutes. The 28-minute difference here is the difference between a tragedy, where every line has significance and is pondered over, and a comedy, in which the actors rush from line to line and there is no time to dwell on the full implications of an incident.

The question of what type of play a drama is also bears on the types of issue the director wants the audience to think about. In order to accentuate certain themes in a play, a director may cut scenes which do not deal with those themes or lengthen the action of scenes in the play that do deal with them. For example, Aphra Behn's *The Rover* can be played as a straightforward bawdy Restoration comedy. In order to accentuate this, Peter Hall cut the opening scene of Behn's script, which involves Florinda and Hellena discussing how to avoid being married and being sent to a convent, and replaced it with the entry of the male Cavaliers into Naples, wondering how to satisfy their sexual appetites. Some critics objected to this, because for them it subverted the focus on women's issues – issues which are particularly important in regard to Behn, who was the first woman to make a living as a playwright.

> **A director will cut certain scenes and accentuate others in order to highlight particular themes.**

## Setting

The issue of where a play is set relates to two factors – time and place. In terms of time, the question of what period of history to set a play in is determined by its relevance to a contemporary audience. A play which is set in the present immediately proclaims its relevance to contemporary society, whereas a play set in the past initiates a distance between the audience and the characters in the play. This does not mean, however, that the effect of either of these strategies is completely straightforward. A play which is set in the past can seem like an historical exercise and thus alienate an audience, making them think that its issues have nothing to do with our own concerns. Alternatively, by alienating the audience in this way it might make them think more clearly about the issues involved, forcing them to think afresh about issues which are too deeply embedded in our daily lives for us to notice them properly. A play such as Arthur Miller's *The Crucible*, for example, actually builds this into the script of the play, setting it 300 years ago in order to offer a fresh perspective on the McCarthy trials. On the other hand, updates of Shakespeare's plays are often based on the hope that the issues they deal with are timeless and can be shown to be timeless by being set in the present.

> **Deciding where and when to set a play influences the effect created.**

Where a play is set also ties into the

question of relevance. So if a play is set in Venice and staged in Melbourne, it does not immediately seem to relate to the audience. In practice, the question of place is usually secondary to that of time and it will only be changed if the periodization of the play is changed too. Indeed, the question of where the play is set also tends to be subservient to where the play is produced. For example, Jean Anouilh produced a version of Sophocles's *Antigone* in Nazi-occupied France, and Athol Fugard produced a version of it in apartheid-era South Africa, and in these productions the trials of Antigone were seen as relating to the trials of the French and the black South Africans respectively under repressive regimes. On the other hand, although it is set in a Nazi-inspired 1930s, Richard Loncraine's film of Shakespeare's *Richard III* had less effect when watched in a safely democratic British cinema in the late twentieth century.

> **It is important not only where and when a play is set, but also where and when it is produced.**

### Mise en scène

The *mise en scène* of a play refers to its scenery and props. The nature of the *mise en scène* will therefore depend to a large degree upon the choice of setting. A production which attempts to highlight the timeless quality of a play's themes, for example, might accentuate this by employing a symbolic rather than a realistic *mise en scène*. However, the *mise en scène* also refers to elements of the stage production such as lighting and music. Playing a sombre violin concerto while a character falls haplessly down stairs, for example, would change the meaning of that fall from farce to pathos.

> **The *mise en scène* of a play refers to its scenery and props and largely depends upon the setting.**

### Acting

Two main features of the way a play is acted affect its meaning – the style of acting and the gestures of the actors. In terms of the style of acting, most plays are acted in what might broadly be called a realistic manner. That is, the actors pretend to be the characters they are playing and they try to conceal the effort of that pretence. The advantage of this approach is that the audience is more likely to empathize with a character and become involved in the trials and tribulations of that character. However, that is also the disadvantage of such an approach. Some directors, such as Stephen Berkoff and Bertolt Brecht, prefer actors to act in a stylized way, showing that they are acting, and sometimes use props, such as face masks, to accentuate the illusory nature of acting. The advantage of doing this is that it alienates the audience and thus forces them to think about the roles that are being played, rather than about individual characters. It is also supposed to turn the

> **Most acting is realistic, but stylized acting can be used to force the audience's attention on to the ideas of the play.**

audience's attention away from being caught up in the plot and more towards the ideas of the play.

It is also worth noting the difference between film and theatre adaptations of plays in this regard. On stage, actors have to make large, dramatic gestures in order for the people at the back to be able to see them, whereas on film, techniques such as camera close-ups allow an actor to make more subtle and realistic gestures to indicate character. Nevertheless, both on stage and on film an actor's gestures can make an enormous difference to the meaning of a play. For example, in Act 3 Scene 4 of Shakespeare's *Hamlet* Polonius hides behind the arras while Gertrude speaks to Hamlet. She then screams for help and Hamlet, upon hearing someone behind the arras, thrusts his sword into it and supposedly unknowingly kills Polonius. If, however, Hamlet looks at the arras when he enters the room and winks at the audience, he indicates by his gesture that he knows Polonius is hiding behind it and that he does not in fact kill him unknowingly.

> **An actor can change the entire meaning of a scene just by the gestures he or she uses.**

**Always ask yourself:**
- ✔ What type of response is the director trying to elicit from the audience and how does this relate to the meaning of the play?
- ✔ What effects are created by the setting and *mise en scène* of the play and how do these aid our understanding of the play?
- ✔ How do the methods and gestures of the actors change the meaning of the play?

# Analysing Shakespearean drama

## 20

*He is perhaps second only to Chaucer in terms of the fear he strikes into the hearts of students. He also combines the two forms of literature with which students tend to find the most difficulty – poetry and drama. And he is almost guaranteed to turn up on an exam paper. He is, of course, William Shakespeare. For some time now Shakespeare has been the pre-eminent author in English Literature. This status looks set to continue and so, in order to help you write about Shakespeare's plays and poetry, this chapter will provide you with a brief overview of some of the issues you need to consider when analysing the work of the Bard.*

## SHAKESPEARE AND HIS THEATRE

Between his baptism on 26 April 1564 and his burial on 25 April 1616, very little is known about the life of William Shakespeare beyond small facts, such as that he bequeathed his wife the second-best bed in his will. We do know, however, that 37 plays are credited to his name and that the wealth he earned from these and from acting enabled him to invest in land, property and the Globe Theatre, in which he held a 10 per cent interest.

The Globe itself was one of the earliest permanent theatres built in Britain. In fact, it was made from the dismantled timber of the first theatre – simply called the Theatre – and like that venue it was built just outside the city walls of London to escape the jurisdiction of the Common Council of London who were responsible for licensing plays. Unlike today, then, a trip to see a Shakespeare play was a trip to the margins of society on a par with, and very often using the same space as, bear-baiting and dog-fighting.

> **Shakespeare's theatre was on the margins of society.**

Also unlike the theatre of today, there was a minimal use of scenery. As painted scenery was not developed until the Restoration, the mood of the play was indicated by the use of a dark curtain for tragedies and lighter and coloured curtains for comedies. Shakespeare therefore had to employ words to set the scene, although there was a limited use of props.

> **Renaissance theatre did not use scenery, so Shakespeare had to describe the scene in words.**

It is also worth noting that there was a far greater interaction between the audience and the actors than we tend to experience today. Actors often entered the stage from the audience in the yard or pit (the non-seated area of the theatre) and they, particularly the comedians, would exchange banter with members of the public.

## THE EFFECTS OF SHAKESPEARE'S THEATRE

The semi-renegade status of Shakespearean theatre was not just a result of its geographical location on the margins of society, but also a result of the effects of the plays themselves. Unlike those of today, Renaissance literary analysts were less concerned with the intrinsic meaning of a text, and more concerned with its effect on an audience. Some held that plays could instruct the audience to know their place and respect their betters. The actor and dramatist Thomas Heywood, for example, argued that by dramatizing 'the untimely end of such as have moved tumults, commotions and insurrections', plays taught 'subjects obedience to their king'. On the other hand, both the king himself, James I, and earlier the queen, Elizabeth I, were worried that the dissolute behaviour of a monarch on stage could become, as James wrote, 'the mother of rebellion and disorder'. Unlike British playwrights today, then, of whom no one takes much notice, Shakespeare had to tread a delicate balance if he did not want to offend those in power.

> **Elizabeth I and James I were both worried that the theatre would cause people to disrespect them.**

## THEMES AND IMAGERY IN SHAKESPEARE'S PLAYS

Although each of Shakespeare's plays has its own set of concerns and imagery, there are themes which run throughout his work. Many of these themes are not just his own, but reflect the interests of the historical context within which they were written.

### Legitimacy

The problem of legitimacy runs throughout Shakespeare's plays, from comedies, such as *Much Ado About Nothing*, to tragedies, such as *Hamlet*. It is such a central concern because it was a topic that had tormented England, and eventually Scotland, for hundreds of years, causing war and disorder on a regular basis as various parties fought to establish the rightful successor to the throne. Shakespeare's history plays are explicitly about this problem, examining the ways in which succession is guaranteed by inheritance, primogeniture, divine right or a mixture of the three. With Elizabeth childless and Parliament pressing her to name a successor, the issue of legitimacy was painfully germane in Shakespeare's day. Indeed, *Richard II*, which shows a legitimate king dethroned, was used in the rebellion led by the Earl of Essex to usurp Elizabeth. After it had failed she complained about the identification of her with Richard II.

> **The biggest political problem in Shakespeare's day was who had the right to be the next monarch.**

## The king's two bodies

Closely linked with the theme of legitimacy is the notion of the king's two bodies. Popular belief during the Renaissance maintained that the monarch was composed of two bodies – the body mystical and the body natural. The body natural was the flesh and bones with which a monarch was born, and the body mystical was the divinely inherited body of the crown which passed from one body natural to another. If this notion is probably at its most striking in the history chronicles, it is also at work in other plays, such as *Hamlet* where the body mystical lives on without the body natural in the form of the King's Ghost. The body also provides Shakespeare with an image of the nation as a whole, having the monarch at its head. Such an image creates an organic link between every member of a state, meaning that if one part of the national body is corrupted then so is the whole. As Rosencrantz in *Hamlet* points out, 'Never alone / Did the King sigh, but with a general groan'.

> **The monarch was said to have two bodies – the body natural and the body mystical.**

## Naturalness

Broadly speaking, in Shakespeare's plays if something is good it is natural and if it is bad it is unnatural. For example, when Othello threatens to kill Desdemona she argues 'That death's unnatural that kills for loving'. Nothing is more natural in Shakespeare's plays than order, so when disorder sets in it is marked by a use of unnatural imagery, such as monstrous births (*Richard III, King Lear, Macbeth*), disease (*Coriolanus, Macbeth, Hamlet*) and the disruption of linear time (*Hamlet, Troilus and Cressida, Macbeth*).

> **In Shakespeare's plays, if something is good it is natural and if it is bad it is unnatural.**

## Theatricality

The image of the stage was a common metaphor in Shakespeare's time, one that both Elizabeth and James, for example, were happy to use. People were accustomed to think of themselves as playing a role. It is unsurprising, then, that Shakespeare's plays, given that they are plays, take up this theme with gusto. In *Henry IV Part 1*, for instance, Hal spends much of his time acting out different roles, such as Hotspur, Hotspur's wife, and his father. Similarly, Iago, in *Othello*, goes through almost the entire play acting the part of a loyal friend and follower.

> **The image of the stage was a common metaphor in Shakespeare's time.**

## Internecine conflict

'Internecine' refers to a conflict within a group or organization and it is a common cause of disorder in Shakespeare's plays. At a micro-level, internecine conflict often takes place within a family, perhaps the most obvious example being in *King Lear*,

> **Shakespeare's plays are often about civil wars within families or states.**

where Goneril and Regan turn against Lear and Edward betrays his father. This micro-level of internal conflict is also usually linked to a macro-level, where a country or state turns against itself in a civil war, as also happens in *King Lear*. Again, the theme of internecine conflict is linked to the problems of the country at the time, with people split between Catholics and Protestants and over who should sit on the throne.

## Carnivalesque

The carnivalesque involves the overturning of the natural order of things. During Renaissance festivals an ordinary person would be elected to the position of Lord of Misrule. The Lord of Misrule would preside over the festival, ridiculing and lampooning senior members of the social hierarchy. Shakespeare's plays, particularly his comedies, are often structured around a carnivalesque subversion of the natural order of things. For example, in *A Midsummer Night's Dream* Bottom's head is turned into an ass, and in *Twelfth Night, or, What You Will* (itself one of the festivals in question) Olivia falls for a woman dressed as a man. Some critics argue that carnivalesque periods of misrule were a rehearsal for the various revolutions imminent at the time. Other critics (including James I) argue that Renaissance festivals were periods of licence in which ordinary people were allowed to let off steam to

> **In Shakespeare's comedies there is often a period of misrule during which the existing hierarchy is overturned.**

*stop* them becoming involved in revolutions. Shakespeare's plays tend to follow the latter argument as the period of misrule invariably ends with order being re-established.

## WRITING ABOUT SHAKESPEARE

When you write about a Shakespeare play:

- Make sure you are using the right edition for your examining board. Shakespeare's plays were only published after his death and they exist in different editions called *quartos* and *folios*. Depending on the play, modern editors of Shakespeare have to choose between several conflicting versions of almost every line. This means that no two editions of a play are exactly the same, so you need to get the right one.
- Check you understand the meaning of every word. Shakespeare employed a vast vocabulary, much of it no longer in use. You therefore need to look up the meaning of obscure words as they can change the sense of what is being said.
- Try to contextualize the play. You can do this in a number of ways. First, you can contextualize the themes of the play in terms of Renaissance history, as I have been doing here. Secondly, you can contextualize the play in terms of Shakespeare's other plays, drawing comparisons between the treatment of similar

themes and topics, such as the portrayal of Rome in *Coriolanus*, *Julius Caesar* and *Antony and Cleopatra*. Thirdly, you can contextualize the play in terms of its source. Shakespeare very often used a published story as a source for his play, such as Giraldi Cinthio's *Hecatommithi* for *Othello*, and where this is the case you can show how Shakespeare altered the story to produce a particular effect. Fourthly, you can contextualize the play in terms of its performance, comparing different versions of it on stage or film and demonstrating how they achieve different effects.

**Always ask yourself:**
- ✔ What is the historical context of the play and how does this context manifest itself?
- ✔ How does the treatment of the play's themes and imagery compare to other Shakespeare plays?
- ✔ How does the performance of the play change its meaning?

# Analysing the structure of poetry (Part 1)

## 21

Poetry, according to the critic Roman Jakobson, 'is organized violence committed on ordinary speech'. This does not mean that poems are created by teams of Mafia assassins taking a chainsaw to the family dictionary, although some poets have been known to exercise their creative temperament in a similar way. Rather, Jakobson's definition draws our attention to two important facts about poetry. First, it is not like ordinary speech, even though it generally uses the same words as ordinary speech. Secondly, it is not like ordinary speech because it is organized in a different, more disturbed or intense arrangement than the sentences we commonly use to converse with each other. This chapter will look at the arrangement of poetry and explain the key terms used to define its structures.

## METRE

Most poetry written in English is structured around the way it sounds. The sound of poetry is based upon the pattern of heavily stressed or accented syllables and lightly stressed or accented syllables in a word, phrase or line. Every word, every sentence and every line with more than one syllable will have contrasting emphases on the different syllables, either strong or weak.
*Metre* is the pattern of contrasting syllabic emphasis.

> **Metre is the pattern of heavily and weakly stressed syllables in a poem.**

*Scansion* is the study of poetry for metre. When you analyse a poem you need to *scan* it line by line for the patterns of syllabic emphasis. These metrical patterns are called *feet*. The most common feet contain either two or three syllables. A heavily stressed syllable is indicated by the mark /, and a weakly stressed syllable is marked by an *x*.

- **Iamb** An iamb is a foot consisting of one weakly stressed syllable followed by one heavily stressed syllable: *x /*. Examples include 'hel*lo*', 'good*bye*' and 'be*hind*'.
- **Trochee** The opposite of an iamb, a trochee is a foot consisting of one strongly stressed syllable followed by one weakly stressed syllable: */ x*. Examples include '*faith*less', '*crea*ture' and '*wea*ver'.
- **Anapaest** An anapaest is a foot consisting of two weakly stressed syllables followed by a strongly stressed syllable: *x x /*. Examples include 'ever*more*', 'under*hand*' and 'milli*gramme*'.

- **Dactyl** The opposite of an anapaest, a dactyl is a foot consisting of one heavily stressed syllable followed by two weakly stressed syllables: / x x. Examples include 'demonize', 'complicate' and 'deviate'.

This is by no means an exclusive list of the available types of metrical feet, but it does contain the ones you are most likely to encounter in the poems you study.

If a line of poetry is split up into feet, the number of feet in that line indicate its length. The number of feet per line also have specific technical names:

- **Monometer** A monometer is a line one foot in length.
- **Dimeter** A dimeter is a line two feet in length.
- **Trimeter** A trimeter is a line three feet in length.
- **Tetrameter** A tetrameter is a line four feet in length.
- **Pentameter** A pentameter is a line five feet in length.
- **Hexameter** A hexameter is a line six feet in length.
- **Heptameter** A heptameter is a line seven feet in length.

When you describe the metre of a line of poetry you need to discern the predominant type of feet and how many are used. For example, Shakespeare's Sonnet 22 is mostly written in iambic pentameter – that is, lines of five feet with alternate weak and strong stressed syllables:

```
x    /   x   /  x   /   x / x  /
My glass/ shall not/ persuade/ me I/ am old
x   /  x   /   x   /  x / x   /
So long/ as youth/ and thou/ are of/ one date;
 x   /  x  /   /   x   x  / x /
But when/ in thee/ time's fur/ rows I /behold,
  x  / x /   x   /   x   /  x /
Then look/ I death/ my days/ should ex/ piate.
```

Andrew Marvell's 'To His Coy Mistress', on the other hand, is written mainly in iambic tetrameter – that is, lines of four feet with alternate weak and strong stressed syllables:

```
 / x   x  /   x  /   x  /
Had we/ but world/ enough/ and time,
 x  /    x  / x  /   x  /
This coy/ ness, la/ dy, were/ no crime.
/   x   x  /   x  /   x   /
We would/ sit down/ and think/ which way
 x  /  x   /  x  /   x   /
To walk/ and pass/ our long/ love's day.
```

The pattern of metrical feet does not respect the boundaries of individual words, as you can see in the third and fourth lines of Shakespeare's sonnet where the iamb cuts across both 'furrows' and 'expiate'. Nor does a poem have to keep rigidly to the same metre throughout. In Marvell's poem, for example, the first feet of lines one and three are actually trochees rather than iambs, but as the poem is largely written using iambs it is iambic.

## RHYME

Another, and perhaps more obvious way in which poetry is organized around its sound is by the use of rhyme. In its most popular form, rhyme denotes the use of similar-sounding words or syllables at the end of a line of verse. It can be seen in this famous example, Robert Herrick's 'To the Virgins, To Make Much of Time':

> Gather ye Rose-buds while ye may,
> Old time is still a-flying:
> And this same flower that smiles today,
> Tomorrow will be dying.

'May' in line one rhymes with 'today' in line three. This type of rhyme is called a *masculine rhyme*. Masculine rhymes are those which fall on heavily stressed syllables (common in most iambic verse). 'Flying' and 'dying' in lines two and four also rhyme. This type of rhyme is called a *feminine rhyme*. Feminine rhymes are those which fall on weakly stressed syllables (common in trochaic verse).

**Masculine rhymes fall on heavily stressed syllables; feminine rhymes fall on weakly stressed syllables.**

Full rhymes like these can exert a form of tyranny over a poem, trivializing the subject matter by compelling the poet to use a word for its sound rather than its sense. In order to avoid this, yet still maintain the sense of aural coherence which rhyme gives a poem, poets have developed the half-rhyme or, as it is technically known, the *pararhyme*. The pararhyme is particularly common in twentieth-century poetry, such as that by Wilfred Owen, W.H. Auden, and in this example, 'The Scholars' by W.B. Yeats:

> Bald heads forgetful of their sins,
> Old learned, respectable bald heads
> Edit and annotate the lines
> That young men, tossing on their beds,
> Rhymed out in love's despair
> To flatter beauty's ignorant ear.

Lines two and four end in conventional masculine rhymes here ('heads' and 'beds'). Lines one and three end with a pararhyme in which the two rhyming words, 'sins' and 'lines', share the 'in' sound but not completely. Similarly, the last two lines here end with a pararhyme between 'despair' and 'ear'. The former word ends with a heavy stress and sets up a rhythmic expectation for the following line, one which is only half met by the weakly stressed second syllable of 'ear', a failure of rhyme which echoes the ignorance of beauty's ear.

**A pararhyme is an imperfect or inexact rhyme.**

Poems can further be analysed according to their *rhyme schemes*. This is done using the alphabet to indicate rhymes of a similar sound. Each new rhyme is given a new letter of the alphabet, as can be seen here in the first stanza of John Donne's 'The Sun Rising':

| | |
|---|---|
| Busy old fool, unruly sun, | **a** |
| Why dost thou thus | **b** |
| Through windows, and through curtains, call on us? | **b** |
| Must to thy motions lovers' seasons run? | **a** |
| Saucy pedantic wretch, go chide | **c** |
| Late school-boys and sour prentices, | **d** |
| Go tell court-huntsmen, that the King will ride, | **c** |
| Call country aunts to harvest offices; | **d** |
| Love, all alike, no season knows, nor clime, | **e** |
| Nor hours, days, months, which are the rags of time. | **e** |

If you were writing about this poem in an essay, you would describe the rhyme scheme as *abbacdcdee*. Donne's poem is typical of poems that use a rhyme scheme in that the stanza ends with an *heroic couplet* – a pair of rhyming lines written in iambic pentameter. When used, as they are here, to end a poem or stanza, heroic couplets tend to mark the conclusion or summing-up of the poem's argument, bringing it to a neat and tidy denouement. Most of Shakespeare's sonnets end with an heroic couplet in this way. Some poets, notably Alexander Pope, wrote whole poems in heroic couplets and in these cases the second line of the couplet usually bears in a witty way on the first line, turning the couplet into a form of epigram.

> **An heroic couplet is a pair of rhyming lines written in iambic pentameter.**

## BLANK VERSE AND FREE VERSE

While many people consider rhyme to be an essential part of a good poem, two important verse forms do not use rhyme schemes – *blank verse* and *free verse*:

- **Blank verse** Blank verse is unrhymed verse written in iambic pentameter. First used in England in 1557 by the Earl of Surrey in his translation of Virgil's *Aeneid*, it has since become the most popular and significant form of verse. Its most notable uses are in Shakespeare's plays, John Milton's *Paradise Lost*, and William Wordsworth's *The Prelude*.

- **Free verse** Free verse is poetry that is neither rhymed nor written in a strict metrical pattern, in terms of either the type or the number of feet used in a line. The only kind of pattern usually discerned in free verse occurs *between* lines of a poem rather than *within* them, most commonly with the use of more heavy stresses in one line followed by a line or lines with less heavy stresses. The most notable exponents of free verse are twentieth-century poets, such as T.S. Eliot, Wallace Stevens and William Carlos Williams.

**Always ask yourself:**
✔ What type of metre does the poem use?
✔ What type of rhymes does the poem use?
✔ What rhyme scheme does the poem use?

# Analysing the structure of poetry (Part 2)

## 22

*If you wish to receive a top grade, it is important when you write about a poem that you are able to identify and name its metre and rhyme. However, now you know what to call the bits and pieces of a poem the question you might well be asking is, 'And?' Those of you who have been reading this book in order will know that the most important part of any essay is analysis, not description. So far I have described the main features of a poem's structure but I have not analysed their effects. This is because even though individual poems may share the same structure, that structure does not necessarily have the same effect in each poem. The effect of a poem's structure is largely dependent on the meaning of the poem itself. There are, however, several conventions which most critics employ when analysing poetry that you can use as guides to help you write about a poem.*

## THE PRINCIPLE OF CORRESPONDENCE

There is no intrinsic link between the structure of a poem and the meaning of the words in that poem. Nevertheless, it is conventional to treat poetry as if there is a link or correspondence between them. When you write about a poem, you need to apply this principle of correspondence and demonstrate how the poem's phonetic arrangement – its sound and metre – underline or undermine its meaning.

> **When you analyse a poem you need to show how the sound and metre of the words correspond to the meaning of the words.**

There are a number of conventions central to the principle of correspondence:

1 Line endings represent spatial or temporal gaps.
2 Words are onomatopoeic – that is, the sounds of words echo their sense.
3 Deviations from the dominant metre within a line of a poem draw attention to a specific word or phrase.
4 Similar-sounding words in a poem forge a connection between those words at the level of meaning.
5 Words represent something more than they mean.

**1 Line endings represent spatial or temporal gaps.** This convention allows that the way a line ends and/or its connection with the line that follows it is in some way imitative of the words that form the lines. There are two main types of line ending – *enjambment* and *end-stopping*.

- **Enjambment** Deriving from the French word for 'straddle', an enjambment is a line of poetry whose meaning runs on into the next line without the use of punctuation. In W.B. Yeats's 'He Hears the Cry of the Sedge', for example, the sense of the first line runs on into the second – 'I wander by the edge / Of this desolate lake'.
- **End-stopping** End-stopping is where the end of the line corresponds with a grammatical pause. In Thomas Love Peacock's 'Seamen Three', for example, the first two lines take the form of a question and answer and are therefore both grammatically distinct and end-stopped – 'Seamen three! What men be ye? / Gotham's three wise men we be.'

Of the two types of line ending, enjambment is the more useful for analytical purposes. In Yeats's 'He Hears the Cry of the Sedge' the enjambment is marked by the word 'edge', a term which is descriptive both of the border of the lake and the end of the line. As the meaning of the first line continues in the next line, we are forced to traverse back round the borders of the poem to read it, imitating the spatial movement of the poetic persona wandering around the edge of the lake. The use of an enjambment to imitate the spatial movement contained in the sense of a word is a common technique in poetry. In John Milton's *Paradise Lost*, for example, Satan's fall from grace is mimicked by the use of an enjambment in the following lines – 'and how he fell / From heaven'. The description of Satan's descent into hell is here matched by the descent from one line to the next.

**2   Words are onomatopoeic.** At its simplest, onomatopoeia designates those words which sound like the noise they are describing, such as 'bang', 'crash' and 'wallop'. The analysis of poetry applies this principle more widely, allowing that the sound of words can also convey a meaning or value. This is called *phonaesthemia*. A *phonaestheme* is a particular sound associated with a group of words. Take a look at the following lines from John Keats's 'Ode on Indolence':

> For Poesy! – no, – she has not a joy, –
> At least for me, – so sweet as drowsy noons,
> And evenings steep'd in honied indolence

It could be argued that Keats employs a number of words here with phonaesthemic resonances. For example, 'drowsy' uses the same '-zy' sound as 'hazy' and 'lazy' which, with their connotations of a vagueness or languidness of spirit, reinforce the sense of indolence conveyed in 'drowsy'.

> **A *phonaestheme* is a particular sound associated with a group of words.**

A similar case could be made for 'noons' and the association of 'oon' sounds in words like 'swoon', 'lagoon' and 'moon'. The truth of the matter is that these associations are rarely pure – for example, 'crazy' contains the 'zy' sound – and so the link is generally a weak one.

**3   Deviations from the dominant metre within a line of a poem draw attention to a specific word or phrase.** If the metre of a poem is its regular pattern of stresses, the rhythm of a poem is the difference between that metre and deviations from it made in the reading of the poem. Wherever the rhythm deviates from the metre, it draws attention to particular words, stressing them for thematic purposes. For example, take a look at the opening two lines of Shakespeare's 'Sonnet XII':

```
x  /  x  /    x  /    x  /  x  /
When I do count the clock that tells the time
x  /  x  /    /  /  x  x  x  /
And see the brave day sunk in hideous night
```

Written in iambic pentameter, the rhythm of the first line sticks as rigidly to the metrical beat as the clock does to the time. This is the objective experience of time – the time of clocks and watches – but as we all know time speeds up or slows down according to our mood. Thus, in the second line, where the experience of day and night becomes more subjective (the day is 'brave' and the night is 'hideous'), the rhythm deviates from its regular metre with an extra heavily stressed syllable on 'day' and a corresponding weaker stress on 'hideous'. (If you are wondering why there are only two accents for 'hideous' it is because I have treated it as a *diphthong*, eliding the two vowel sounds to pronounce it 'hid-jus'.) The effect of this extra heavy stress is to accentuate the word 'sunk' so that the rhythm of the line

> **Metre is the dominant pattern of stresses in a poem, whereas rhythm is the actual pattern of stresses used when it is read.**

metaphorically sinks down on the word 'in', thus reinforcing the meaning of the words.

There are three main ways in which the regular metre of a line of poetry is altered – by *demotion, promotion* or *caesura*.

- **Demotion** A syllable is demoted when a heavily stressed syllable becomes a weakly stressed syllable.
- **Promotion** A syllable is promoted when a weakly stressed syllable becomes a heavily stressed syllable.
- **Caesura** A caesura is a grammatical pause in the middle of a line which disrupts the line's metre. It is commonly indicated by the use of strong punctuation, such as the exclamation mark in the first line of William Wordsworth's 'To the Cuckoo' – 'O blithe New-comer! I have heard, / I hear thee and rejoice.'

**4   Similar-sounding words in a poem forge a connection between those words at the level of meaning.** There are five principal ways of classifying the sounds of words in poetry – *alliteration* and *consonance, assonance, euphony* and *cacophony*.

- **Alliteration and consonance** Alliteration refers to the repetition of consonants, particularly at the beginning of words or on syllables with a heavy stress.

For example, in Wallace Stevens's 'A High-Toned Old Christian Woman' the last two lines are held together by the alliteration of the letter 'w' – 'This will make widows wince: But fictive things / Wink as they will. Wink most when widows wince.' Consonance is a more precise form of alliteration which refers to words where the consonants are the same but the vowels are different, such as 'pat', 'pet', 'pit', 'pot' and 'put'.

- **Assonance**  Assonance refers to the repetition of vowel sounds. In the first line of John Keats's 'Ode on Indolence', for example – 'One morn before me were three figures seen' – the 'e' is assonantal in 'b<u>e</u>fore', 'm<u>e</u>', 'thr<u>ee</u>' and 's<u>een</u>'.
- **Euphony and cacophony**  Euphony refers to an arrangement of words that is harmonious or pleasing to the ear. Cacophony is the opposite of euphony and refers to an arrangement of words which is discordant or jars on the ear. As you might imagine, this is a rather subjective way of appraising sound. Samuel Coleridge's 'Frost at Midnight', for example, begins with the lines – 'The frost performs its secret ministry, / Unhelped by any wind'. Some people might find the repetition of the clipped sounds of the 'r's with the 'f's and 't's here a harmonious or euphonious arrangement, while others might hear the sounds as overly staccato or cacophonous.

Connections between the sounds of words create a link between those words at the level of meaning. Returning to the alliteration in Stevens's 'A High-Toned Old Christian Woman', for example, a link is forged between 'wink' and 'wince' by the 'wi-' sound. This might seem strange given that a 'wink' is an act of intimacy and a 'wince' is a withdrawal from intimacy, yet the alliteration of the two words underlines their sameness in a way that using, say, 'recoil' for 'wince' would not have done. This corresponds to the pattern of the poem as a whole, the theme of which is that religion and poetry share many features in common. In the poem, 'wincing' belongs to religion and 'winking' belongs to poetry. The alliteration of the 'wi' sound helps to unify these two different types of discourse, highlighting their formal similarity rather than their difference.

    **5    Words represent something more than they mean.**  Poets sometimes take advantage of the fact that words are made up of both a sound and a meaning by highlighting a word's phonetic qualities at the expense of its sense. This is done for two main reasons. Either it indicates a failure of words adequately to express an emotion, such as a sublime feeling, or it indicates a delight in words for the sounds they make, such as may be found in the nonsense poems of Edward Lear or even Dr Seuss. Returning to Stevens's 'A High-Toned Old Christian Woman', for example, we can see both elements at work in the lines 'Proud of such novelties of the sublime, / Such tink and tank and tunk-a-tunk-tunk'. The words in the last line are more or less meaningless, but they convey a childish delight in their own sounds.

> **Words are sometimes used for the way they sound rather than for what they mean.**

As the first line suggests, these words are also a way of representing a feeling of sublimity – a feeling which, by definition, is beyond the power of words to express.

The only way to express that feeling, then, is by using words which do not mean anything.

**Always ask yourself:**
✔ How does the structure of the poem reinforce the meaning of its words?
✔ In what ways do the arrangement and sounds of the words imitate the meaning of the words?
✔ In what ways do the arrangement and sounds of the words create a pattern that links the words together?

## 23

*Poetry is often thought of as the most privileged of the literary genres. This is because it is more specifically literary than either drama or the novel, more clearly different from everyday ways of communicating. As we have seen already, this difference mainly proceeds from the phonetic arrangement of poetry – the way its sounds are organized into patterns. However, in addition to this, poetry tends to use more figurative language than either ordinary discourse or even other literary genres. When you analyse a poem, you need to name and explain the different rhetorical figures that it uses. In order to help you* do that, this chapter will identify some of the more common figures of speech, or types of poetic language, and clarify what they mean.

## THE ROLE OF POETIC FIGURATION

Although some poems tell stories, they tend to be concerned with describing the development of a single thought, feeling or situation. Description therefore tends to predominate over action. The importance of description to poetry means that it tends to employ more figures of speech, or figuration, in order to create fresh ways of looking at the world. I have already detailed the most basic forms of figuration in Chapter 11. In this chapter I have divided some of the remaining rhetorical figures you will encounter into three types – figures of *anthropomorphism*, figures of *contradiction and comparison*, and figures of *repetition and reversal*. This chapter will also look at *deictics*, or the orientational features of a poem.

### Figures of anthropomorphism

One of the most common types of rhetorical figure in poetry, anthropomorphism is a way of referring to animals, things, ideas or even God in human terms. There are three main types of anthropomorphism which are only subtly different – *personification*, *animism* and *hypostatization*.

- **Personification** Personification refers to the process of giving human characteristics to an animal, thing or idea. One thing that is regularly personified in poetry is death, which, when you think about it, is very strange given that it is really an absence of life. One of the most famous examples of this is Emily Dickinson's 'Because I Could Not Stop for Death':

  > Because I could not stop for Death –
  > He kindly stopped for me –
  > The Carriage held but just Ourselves –
  > And Immortality.

- **Animism** Animism refers to the rhetorical figure which attributes a spirit or form of life to things or inanimate objects. This effect is usually achieved by attributing verbs or actions for the objects to perform. For instance, in Philip Larkin's 'At Grass', the fieldglass is described as if it had the independent ability to see – 'And not a fieldglass sees them home'. Animism is sometimes also applied to the natural world. In Alfred Tennyson's 'The Dying Swan', for example, the whole of a riverbank is brought to life:

> And the *creeping* mosses and *clambering* weeds,
> And the willow branches hoar and dank,
> And the wavy smell of the *soughing* reeds,
> And the wave-worn horns of the *echoing* bank,
> And the silvery marish-flowers that *throng*
> The desolate creeks and pools among,
> Were flooded over with eddying song.

- **Hypostatization** Hypostatization is a way of referring to abstract qualities as though they were endowed with life. In the first line of William Wordsworth's 'Mutability', for example, 'From low to high doth dissolution climb', 'dissolution' is referred to as if it were an independent entity that could perform the action of 'climbing'.

Anthropomorphism tends to produce two contradictory effects. On the one hand, it makes the non-human world – the world of animals and things – more human-like and therefore more familiar to us. On the other hand, by giving human attributes to the non-human, anthropomorphism estranges those attributes, making them seem oddly unfamiliar. In literary criticism, this double effect comes under the name of the *uncanny*. The uncanny is the English translation of the German word '*unheimlich*' which means 'unhomely'. The uncanny refers to a way of looking at the world which finds the familiar in the unfamiliar and, conversely, the unfamiliar in the familiar.

> **Anthropomorphism tends to produce two contradictory effects: it makes the familiar strange and the strange familiar.**

Perhaps the ultimate rhetorical figure of the unfamiliar in the familiar is the exact opposite of anthropomorphism, which is *automatism*.

- **Automatism** Automatism is a way of describing humans in non-human terms, usually mechanical ones. In Samuel Coleridge's *The Rime of the Ancient Mariner*, for example, the Ancient Mariner describes the crew's bodies in mechanistic terms – 'They raised their limbs like lifeless tools'.

### Figures of contradiction and comparison

Every figure of speech which compares one thing with another is at some level a contradiction in so far as the two things are not exactly alike. If we say that someone has a sunny smile, for example, we mean to imply that the smile is warm. We do not mean to imply that the smile is a flaming ball of gas 333,000 times the size of the Earth. In other words, the sun and the smile are not exactly alike but we understand the comparison in terms of its similarities rather than its differences. Some rhetorical figures, however, tend to highlight the differences in a comparison rather than the similarities.

> **Some rhetorical figures tend to highlight the differences in a comparison rather than the similarities.**

There are three main figures which do this – the *conceit*, the *oxymoron* and *synaesthesia*.

* **Conceit** A conceit is a far-fetched or extravagant comparison between two things which often seem so dissimilar as to make the comparison a contradiction. Perhaps the most famous example of a conceit is John Donne's comparison of love with a pair of compasses in 'A Valediction Forbidding Mourning':

> If they be two, they are two so
> As stiff twin compasses are two,
> Thy soul the fixed foot, makes no show
> To move, but doth, if th'other do.

* **Oxymoron** An oxymoron is a figure of speech which brings together seemingly opposing terms. D.H. Lawrence's 'Tortoise Shout', for example, is based on a fundamental opposition, that between part and whole: 'That which is whole, torn asunder, / That which is in part, finding its whole again throughout the universe'.
* **Synaesthesia** Synaesthesia is the description of one type of sensory impression in terms more traditionally associated with another type of sensory impression. In Percy Shelley's 'Ode to the West Wind', for example, the lines 'All overgrown with azure moss and flowers / So sweet, the sense faints picturing them!' mix the sense of taste ('sweet') with that of vision ('picturing').

### Figures of repetition and reversal

If one of the effects of poetry's extensive use of rhetorical figures is to make it different from ordinary language, then this is partly achieved by figures which reverse the conventional order of words. A reversal in word order is also a form of repetition, what is called a repetition with a difference, because it can only be a reverse of something if it in some way alludes to, or mimics, what it changes.

> **Merely by reversing the conventional word order of a phrase, a poem can make a thought, feeling or experience seem fresh.**

The main figures of repetition and reversal are *anaphora*, *chiasmus*, *hypallage* and *hyperbaton*.

* **Anaphora** An anaphora is a type of refrain in which phrases or words are repeated in successive clauses or verses. Part V of W.B. Yeats's 'Nineteen

Hundred and Nineteen', for example, is structured around the following anaphora – 'Come let us mock at the great', 'Come let us mock at the wise', 'Come let us mock at the good'.

*   **Chiasmus** A chiasmus is the repetition of a phrase or series of words in inverted order. In George Byron's *Don Juan*, for example, it is argued that 'Pleasure's a sin, and sometimes sin's a pleasure'. Poetry also lends itself particularly well to phonetic chiasmus, or a reversal of sounds. For example, in Samuel Coleridge's 'Xanadu', the opening line contains a reversal of the 'an' and 'oo' sounds – 'In Xanadu, did Kubla Khan'. In addition, a chiasmus can refer more generally to the reversal of an idea. In Percy Shelley's 'Song to the Men of England', for example, the poem uses a chiasmus to propose a quasi-revolutionary attitude, contrasting an existing state of affairs with a command to change it:

> The seed ye sow, another reaps:
> The wealth ye find, another keeps;
> The robes ye weave, another wears;
> The arms ye forge, another bears.
>
> Sow seed, – but let no tyrant reap;
> Find wealth, – let no impostor heap;
> Weave robes, – let not the idle wear;
> Forge arms, – in your defence to bear.

*   **Hypallage** A hypallage is a phrase in which the natural relations between two words are interchanged. For example, in the first line of John Keats's *Hyperion* – 'Deep in the shady sadness of a vale' – it is really the 'vale' that is 'shady' but the adjective is used here to describe the 'sadness'.
*   **Hyperbaton** A hyperbaton refers to the reversal or inversion of normal word order. In Alexander Pope's 'Elegy to the Memory of an Unfortunate Lady', for example, the line 'Like Eastern Kings a lazy state they keep' reverses the natural order in English of 'subject-predicate' – 'they keep a lazy state'.

### Deictics

Deictics are the orientational features of a poem. They tell you who is speaking, where and when they are speaking from and to whom they are speaking.

Deictics include *pronouns, articles, words of place and time*, and *verb tenses*.

*   **Pronouns** Pronouns are words that stand in for nouns that have been or will be mentioned, such as 'it', 'she' and 'they'. Pronouns are particularly important in poetry because we tend to build the poem's *persona* around them. The persona of a poem is the voice of the poem, the one who provides it with a coherent view-point. The majority of poetic personas are 'I's either thinking to

> **Deictics are the orientational words in a poem – they set it in a place and a time and identify the speaker.**

themselves or addressing another person. William Wordsworth's poem 'Lines Written in Early Spring', for example, is written from the point of view of an 'I' reminding himself of the joys of nature – 'And I must think, do all I can / That there was pleasure there'.

- **Articles** Articles are determiners indicating the specificity of a noun, which may sound complicated but they are basically just 'a' and 'the'. The reason that 'a' and 'the' are important is because they indicate whether something referred to is general – 'a' – or specific – 'the'. In William Blake's 'The Sick Rose', for example, 'The invisible worm' in the second line is a specific worm because it is prefixed by the word 'the' rather than 'an'.

- **Words of place and time** Words such as 'here', 'now' and 'then' indicate a relation of time and place. It is a convention of poetry that words like these can be understood as referring to both a specific time and place and to a more general time and place. In this way, a concrete situation is used as an example of a comment with wider applications. The first line of Fleur Adcock's 'Turnip-Heads', for instance, begins with a reference to a specific 'here' – 'Here are the ploughed fields of Middle England'. As the poem develops we understand that these are the specific fields the poem's persona sees out of a train window. However, the poem also goes on to widen the time-frame to include a consideration of history from the Middle Ages to the present. The fields, the immediate 'here', can therefore be read as representative of England generally in the present.

- **Verb tenses** Most poems are written either in the present or the past tense. In general a poem written in the present tense conveys an immediacy of thinking, while a poem written in the past tense demonstrates a more reflective cast of thought, one where the subject matter is mediated by time. Sometimes the two are combined to great effect. In William Wordsworth's 'Intimations of Immortality', for example, an explicit contrast is made between the glories of the past and the mundaneness of the present – 'It is not now as it hath been of yore'.

### Always ask yourself:
- ✔ What figures of anthropomorphism does the poem use and with what effect?
- ✔ What figures of comparison and repetition does the poem use and with what effect?
- ✔ What deictics does the poem use and with what effect?

# Analysing the meaning of a poem

## 24

According to the poet Samuel Coleridge, a good poem is one 'the parts of which mutually support and explain each other'. What Coleridge means by this is that the different aspects of a poem, such as the imagery, the rhyme scheme, the metre and rhythm, the deictics, and so on, all work together to produce the overarching meaning of the poem. In other words, the validity of one aspect of a poem is determined by its relationship to your analysis of the poem's overall sense. When you analyse a poem, therefore, you need to demonstrate the connection between its different parts and your interpretation of its meaning. To help you do this, this chapter considers in depth a single poem, showing you an example of a way in which you can break a poem down into its different parts and then connect them with each other.

## THE THREE-STEP METHOD FOR ANALYSING A POEM

When you write about a poem you need a strategy for analysing it. The simplest and usually the most effective strategy involves three steps, moving from whole to part to whole.

**Step 1** **Whole** Read the poem all the way through as often as it takes for you to get a basic understanding of what the poem is about. Most poems centre around a conflict, between either two ideas or two ways of thinking about something, resolving that conflict one way or the other at the end.

**Step 2** **Part** Once you have determined the central themes of the poem you need to dismember it, breaking it down into three main areas – *rhyme and metre*, *tone and imagery*, and *deictics*. Trace the development of each of these three areas through the poem, noting, for example, if there are any significant changes in the rhythm or the kind of imagery used.

**Step 3** **Whole** Once you have considered each of the three areas separately, you need to reassemble them to show how they each contribute to the meaning of the poem. At this stage you may need to revise your initial understanding of the poem, demonstrating how a first reading is altered by a more considered analysis. Once you have completed this step you are then ready to plan and write your essay.

Try following this three-step approach with the following poem: 'The Darkling

> **The best way to analyse a poem is to read it as whole, break it down into its parts and then show how the parts relate to the whole.**

Thrush' by Thomas Hardy. When you have done that, compare your notes on the three main areas of the poem with mine, and then see how your interpretation of the meaning of the poem compares with the extracts from two essays discussing the same subject.

## The Darkling Thrush

I leant upon a coppice gate
When Frost was spectre-grey,
And Winter's dregs made desolate
The weakening eye of day.
The tangled bine-stems scored the sky
Like strings of broken lyres,
And all mankind that haunted nigh
Had sought their household fires.

The land's sharp features seemed to be
The Century's corpse outleant,
His crypt the cloudy canopy,
The wind his death-lament.
The ancient pulse of germ and birth
Was shrunken hard and dry,
And every spirit upon earth
Seemed fervourless as I.

At once a voice arose among
The bleak twigs overhead
In a full-hearted evensong
Of joy illimited;
An aged thrush, frail, gaunt, and small,
In blast-beruffled plume,
Had chosen thus to fling his soul
Upon the growing gloom.

So little cause for carollings
Of such ecstatic sound
Was written on terrestrial things
Afar or nigh around,
That I could think there trembled through
His happy good-night air
Some blessed Hope, whereof he knew
And I was unaware.

### Step 1: Whole
On a first reading, the poem seems to be about the conflict between despair and hope. It begins with the poem's persona in a state of despair but, with the introduction of the thrush of the title, it ends with a sense of hope.

## Step 2: Part

*Rhyme and metre*
The poem is arranged in lines of alternate iambic tetrameters and trimeters with a rhyme scheme for each stanza of ababcdcd. What is interesting is that in terms of the syntax and rhythm of the poem the lines are written in heptameters with a rhyme scheme of aabb – more commonly known as rhyming couplets. The rhyme on the last iamb of each tetrameter in its current arrangement then becomes an internal rhyme, pinning the poem down to a very rigid and unrelenting sense of rhythm. Neither the rhythm or the rhyme scheme changes to any great degree whatever the words are saying.

*Tone and imagery*
The tone of the poem is initially bleak. It is riddled with adjectives, such as 'desolate', 'broken', 'fervourless', 'bleak' and 'blast-beruffled', and nouns, such as 'dregs' and 'gloom', which are suggestive of a barren and forlorn feeling. This sense of desolation is underwritten by images and intimations of death, such as the 'spectre-grey' frost, 'the weakening eye of day', the 'Century's corpse', the 'crypt' and the 'death-lament' of the wind. Nor is this a death which countenances the chance of either an afterlife or a regenerative cycle; rather it is a complete and final death where the 'ancient pulse of germ and birth' is 'shrunken hard and dry'. Against this apocalyptic background the song of the thrush is a kind of thematic chiasmus, seeming to offer some form of 'blessed Hope', but it is a hope of which the poem's persona remains 'unaware'. Indeed, the way in which the thrush is said 'to fling his soul / Upon the growing gloom' is redolent of the final ecstasy of a suicide where someone throws him or herself off a building.

*Deictics*
The spatial deictics of the poem are both specific and non-specific. We know, for example, that the poem is ostensibly based near a coppice and therefore in the countryside, but the particular identity of the countryside is unknown. What is more identifiable is the time of the poem, partly because time plays a more important role. The poem is set, for example, in winter and in the evening, both of which are traditionally suggestive of matters drawing to a close. This sense of closure is augmented by the reference to the 'Century's corpse'. The poem was written in 1900 and it seems to be referring to the end of the nineteenth century and the hopes, or lack of them, for the new century.

What is interesting is the link between the poetic persona – the 'I' of the poem – and the sense of the end of time. For just as the persona is '*leant*' upon the gate, so too the 'Century's corpse' is 'out*leant*'. This deliberate link between the death of the century and the poetic persona suggests that the persona too thinks he or she is on the verge of death. This is a suggestion which is underlined by the fact that the century's death is the persona's *own* vision – 'The land's sharp features *seemed* to be / The Century's corpse outleant'. The persona sees the clouds as a metaphoric 'crypt' and hears the wind as a metaphoric 'death-lament'. Furthermore, by person-ifying the century, albeit as a corpse, the poem's persona is making it more human-like and therefore more like him or herself. So, just as the century is dead, the persona is like a corpse in being 'fervourless' and 'unaware' of hope, that is, of a future.

## Step 3: Whole

How do these three elements – the rhyme and metre, the imagery and tone, and the deictics – combine to produce the meaning of the poem? In order to find out, take a look at the following extracts from two essays which tackle the question, 'Discuss the meaning of Thomas Hardy's poem "The Darkling Thrush", paying close attention to its imagery and structure'. See if you can determine which is the better answer and what makes it a better answer.

 **A)** Thomas Hardy's 'The Darkling Thrush' is a poem about the triumph of hope over adversity. The poem is composed of four stanzas of alternating iambic tetrameters and iambic trimeters. The rhyme scheme is ababcdcd in each stanza. The poem begins by describing a winter landscape in which the sun is personified as the 'weakening eye of day' as if its sight is failing. The century is also personified as a dead body. These are unhappy images which leave Thomas Hardy feeling 'fervourless'. Eventually, in the third stanza, the voice of the thrush arises among 'The bleak twigs overhead / In a full-hearted even-song / Of joy illimited'. This happy image contrasts with the previous sad images. Even though the thrush has 'So little cause for carollings' it sings anyway in a moment of blind optimism. This gives Thomas Hardy 'Some blessed Hope' of which he was previously 'unaware'. The poem therefore ends on a happy note, with hope for the future triumphing over the adversity of the winter landscape.

 **B)** The meaning of the poem centres around the tension between the 'blessed Hope' of the thrush's song and the relentless desola-tion of the landscape as seen by the poem's persona. It might seem initially as if the thrush's song is triumphant. This can be seen in the devel-opment of the images of sound in the poem. In the first stanza, the aural landscape is discordant ('the strings of broken lyres'), and in the second stanza it is more harmonious but still depressing ('his death-lament'). The arrival of the thrush in the third stanza, however, creates a chiasmus in the mood as the sound is not only harmonious ('evensong'), but happy too ('Of joy illimited'), a feature which in the final stanza reaches the heights of the 'ecstatic sound' of 'carollings' which herald the birth of Christ. Nevertheless, in spite of this, the outlook for the persona remains bleak as he is 'unaware' of the reason for 'Hope'. Such bleakness is emphasized both by the sense of inevitability produced by the rhyming couplets of the poem and by the unchanging iambic stress pattern, neither of which deviates from the beginning of the poem to the end, so not changing the poem's mood. As the poem is written in the past tense, it can also be assumed that had the 'Hope' come to fruition the ending would have been changed to take account of that.

Can you see that Essay B is better than Essay A? There are several differences between them:

- Essay A describes the metre and rhyme scheme of the poem in more detail than Essay B, but it does not explain the relationship between these and the meaning of the poem. Essay B, on the other hand, uses an analysis of the metre and rhyme scheme to offer a more compelling explanation of the poem's meaning.
- Essay A describes some of the imagery but the analysis is rather random and too much of the poem is quoted without analysis. Essay B, however, picks a set of images, in this case relating to sound, and traces its development throughout the 'The Darkling Thrush', showing how this development contributes to the overall meaning of the poem.
- Essay A manages to contextualize the poem in terms of some of its deictics but it does make an error in assuming the poem's persona to be Thomas Hardy. Essay B makes a far more penetrating analysis of the poem's deictics, particularly in terms of the verb tense it is written in, a tense which radically alters our understanding of the poem's central conflict between hope and despair.

**Always ask yourself:**
✔ What themes and conflicts does the poem initially seem to be about?
✔ What are the poem's rhyme scheme and rhythm, tone and imagery, and deictics, and how do they develop throughout the poem?
✔ How does an analysis of the poem's rhyme scheme and rhythm, tone and imagery, and deictics contribute to the meaning of the poem, changing my initial understanding of it?

*When you analyse a poem you need to be able to contextualize it. The context of a poem includes the historical conditions under which it was written, the particular intertexts it draws upon or quotes, as well as the school and type of poetry to which it belongs. In order to help you contextualize poems, this chapter will look at some of the different types of poetry, explaining their basic themes and some of the more important techniques that they use.*

## DIFFERENT TYPES OF POETRY

Poetry is often defined in terms of what are called 'schools'. These schools are usually no more than loose affiliations between poets, describing the tendency of the poets to use similar techniques or explore similar themes. This should be borne in mind when you read the following descriptions because, on the whole, the poets themselves did not sign up to a particular way of writing poetry; rather it is literary critics who have spotted resemblances between them and so grouped them together. These schools of poetry are, then, more likely to be the result of the influence of an historical context than of a deliberate undertaking by the individual poets to copy each other.

> **Many poems belong to general trends in poetry called schools of poetry.**

### Metaphysical poetry

*Who are its chief exponents?*
The Metaphysicals were seventeenth-century poets, including Richard Crashaw, John Donne, George Herbert, Andrew Marvell and Henry Vaughan.

*What does 'metaphysical' mean?*
The term 'metaphysical' has long been a branch of philosophy concerned with the non-physical world. The poet and playwright John Dryden originally used the term to criticize Donne's poetry, implying that his poems were deliberately esoteric and affected. Dr Johnson picked up on this and applied the epithet to all the poets who wrote like Donne.

*What are Metaphysical poetry's most common techniques?*
The Metaphysicals are most famous for their use of conceits – elaborate images composed of far-fetched comparisons. Their poems are also typically trying to persuade someone of something, and to do this they use wit and wild flights of

logic, drawing on incongruous fields of knowledge, such as astronomy, religion and geometry.

*What are Metaphysical poetry's most common themes?*
Some of the Metaphysical poets, such as Vaughan and Herbert, devoted most of their work to religious themes, whereas Donne and Marvell also looked at themes of love, sex and politics.

> **The major Metaphysical poets, such as Donne and Marvell, are famous for their use of conceits.**

*What is an archetypal Metaphysical poem?*
John Donne's 'A Valediction: Forbidding Mourning'.

## Romantic poetry

*Who are its chief exponents?*
The Romantics were poets writing roughly from the end of the eighteenth century to a third of the way through the nineteenth century, including George Byron, Samuel Coleridge, John Keats, Percy Shelley and William Wordsworth. Although he wrote at the same time and about similar themes, William Blake is not always considered a fully-fledged Romantic because his poetic vision is so individual.

*To what does 'Romantic' refer?*
In this context, 'Romantic' needs to be seen as a reaction against the Augustan Age which preceded this period in history. The Augustans, such as Alexander Pope, Dr Johnson and, earlier, John Dryden, were understood by the Romantics to have valued science, reason and sophisticated society, and used polished wit, strict verse forms and a standard poetic vocabulary. Wordsworth's infamous definition of poetry as a 'spontaneous overflow of powerful feelings' is a direct response to these concerns, championing emotion

> **Wordsworth defined Romantic poetry as a 'spontaneous overflow of powerful feelings'.**

over intellect, the imagination over reason, common language over poetic diction and a general freedom from artificial constraints.

*What are Romantic poetry's most common techniques?*
The Romantics are most notable for their use of lyrical imagery and for breaking away from the more rigid poetical rules of their immediate predecessors. This is not to say that the Romantics did not use established verse forms. Indeed, one of the three dominant types of blank verse in English poetry is named after Wordsworth – one that uses a preponderance of light stresses. (The other two are named after Shakespeare and Milton.)

*What are Romantics poetry's most common themes?*
The Romantics are very different poets but they share certain themes, including nature (particularly versus the corruption of the city), the sublime (where the imagination

exceeds reason) and, most of all, themselves. The beginning of the nineteenth century saw an upsurge in individualism, partly motivated by the libertarian aspects of the French Revolution, and the Romantics were keen to explore this fast-developing notion of the self, specifically in terms of memory, perception and the ability of the individual to shape the world around them.

> **Romantic poetry tends to focus on an exploration of the self, particularly a person's memory and imagination.**

*What is an archetypal Romantic poem?*
William Wordsworth's *The Prelude*.

### Modernist poetry

*Who are its chief exponents?*
Modernist poetry was part of a wider artistic movement known as modernism which dominated the arts for the first fifty years or so of the twentieth century. The most notable poets of this period are T.S. Eliot, Ezra Pound, William Carlos Williams and W.B. Yeats.

*Why is the movement called 'modernism'?*
Modernism refers to the way in which people, for the first time, defined the age in terms of its newness. Previously, people had defined different epochs in the more substantive terms of a temperamental difference, such as Romanticism or the Age of Reason.

*What are modernism's most common techniques?*
As there was no dominant outlook, other than a regard for innovation, modernism is defined more by its multitude of individual styles. However, as part of this, Modernist poets did develop the use of free verse forms.

*What are modernism's most common themes?*
Modernist poetry focuses on the alienation and fragmentation of modern society, a fragmentation that it then attempts to unify using ancient myths from cultures all around the world. Modernist poetry therefore tends to be rather prosaic, detailing the mundaneness of ordinary life, at the same time as being rather esoteric, drawing on references that most people have never heard of, let alone read.

*What is an archetypal Modernist poem?*
T.S. Eliot's *The Waste Land*.

> **Modernist poets, such as T.S. Eliot and W.B. Yeats, use myths to unify their descriptions of modern society.**

### Confessional poetry

*Who are its chief exponents?*
The Confessionals are mainly American poets writing in the middle to late twentieth century, such as John Berryman, Robert Lowell, Sylvia Plath, Anne Sexton and Theodore Roethke.

*Why 'Confessional'?*
These poets are so called because their poetry is highly personal. In this sense it is a reaction against the cult of impersonality enforced by the influential poet and critic

T.S. Eliot, who had argued, earlier in the century, that poetry should be an escape from the self and its emotions.

*What are Confessional poetry's most common techniques?*
The Confessionals are perhaps the most disparate of the schools of poetry considered here, but in the context of the twentieth century perhaps their most telling technique was the reintroduction of the first-person poem.

*What are Confessional poetry's most common themes?*
Like the Romantics, the Confessionals take the self as their most common theme, but this is a specific self rather than an abstract idea of an individual. Confessional poetry therefore tends to seem more biographical or even autobiographical, detailing particular events and the emotions that accompanied them.

> **Confessional poets, such as Sylvia Plath and Anne Sexton, tend to write about specific personal experiences.**

*What is an archetypal Confessional poem?*
Sylvia Plath's 'Daddy'.

### WRITING ABOUT DIFFERENT TYPES OF POETRY

The above list is by no means an exclusive account of the different schools of poetry, but what it does show are certain tendencies in the development of poetry. Most of these types of poetry, for example, are in part based on a reaction against a previous school of poetry, changing the established norm of poetic writing. In this sense, poems can be thought of as a form of reply or response, one which cannot be completely understood in isolation. When you write about a particular poem you should try and discern its relationship with these other types of poetry. You should also try to point out instances where poets have been influenced by previous schools of poetry. So, if you are analysing T.S. Eliot's 'The Love Song of J. Alfred Prufrock', for example, you might point to the influence of the Metaphysical conceit in the image of the evening 'spread out against the sky / Like a patient etherised upon a table'. Of course, the best way to augment your understanding of the poems you are studying is to read as much poetry as you can.

> **When you write about a poem you should try to understand it in terms of the influence of other types of poetry on it.**

#### Always ask yourself:
✔ Does the poem 'belong' to a particular school of poetry and, if so, what are the characteristics of that school which it uses?
✔ In what ways is the poem a response to a previous school of poetry?
✔ In what ways does the poem show the influence of a theme or technique from a previous school of poetry?

# Analysing the structure of novels

*All novels are structured by narratives. A narrative is a representation of a story or series of events in a temporal sequence. If this sounds either deceptively simple or overly complex then that is because it covers everything from the sentence 'Mrs Jenkinson went to the shops and bought a pair of curtains' to Margaret Atwood's* The Handmaid's Tale. *Because of this broad remit, the study of narrative, or narratology, has produced a series of insights over the past few decades which have refreshed our understanding of the structure of novels. This chapter will look at some of the most valuable of these insights.*

## EVENTS

Events are the fundamental units of narratives. At a basic level, if something happens it is an event. This could mean scratching your head or setting fire to it. One obviously has more effect than the other, so in order to make the concept of an event slightly more useful, critics distinguish between *kernels* and *catalysts*.

- **Kernel** A kernel is an event that advances the action by introducing a possibility or opening up an alternative. For example, when Joe declares his love to Dolly in Charles Dickens's *Barnaby Rudge*, she can either accept it or reject it. If she accepts it, he stays, and if she rejects it he joins the army.
- **Catalyst** A catalyst is an event that amplifies, maintains or delays a kernel. For example, the hours that Joe spends wandering around London, eating sandwiches and feeling sorry for himself, before he plucks up courage to declare his love for Dolly, are catalysts.

Kernels form the skeletal structure of a novel, whereas catalysts flesh it out. This is not to say that catalysts are necessarily secondary to kernels. For example, the kernel of Jane Austen's *Pride and Prejudice* is essentially whether or not Elizabeth will marry Darcy; however, given that the outcome of this is not really in doubt, our enjoyment comes from the catalysts, the many ways in which the marriage is delayed.

## CAUSES

Events in novels usually have a cause. Critics distinguish between two different types of causality, as a function either of mimesis (the imitation or representation of real life) or of structure.

- **Mimetic causality** Mimetic causality is an explanation of the cause of an event in terms of why it might happen in real life. For example, Tom and Gatsby in F. Scott Fitzgerald's *The Great Gatsby* swap cars because they are trying to impress each other with their wealth.

*   **Structural causality** Structural causality is an explanation of the cause of an event in terms of the requirements of the plot. For example, Fitzgerald makes Tom and Gatsby swap cars so that Wilson sees Gatsby's car and believes Gatsby to be driving it when it kills his wife, thus providing him with a motive to kill Gatsby.

As you can see here, an event may be caused mimetically and structurally at one and the same time. We tend to experience plots as contrived when the mimetic cause seems like a pretext for the structural cause – as in some horror films, where the reason given for a group splitting up in the middle of a haunted house is really just a pretext for them getting murdered one by one. Some readers experience something of this dissatisfaction when analysing novels, those of Thomas Hardy for example, where Fate is called upon to bring two people together in improbable circumstances.

> **We tend to experience plots as contrived when the mimetic cause seems like a pretext for the structural cause.**

## STORY AND DISCOURSE

One way of dividing the structure of a novel is by the complementary categories of *story* and *discourse*, categories originally introduced by the linguist Emile Benveniste.

*   **Story** A story is a sequence of events or what is represented in a novel. For example, 'The king died and then the queen died' is a story.
*   **Discourse** A discourse is the way in which a story is organized or how it is represented. For example, the discourse of the story 'The king died and then the queen died' is ordered in chronological progression and told from a third-person point of view.

Discourse has two main components – point of view, or the perspective from which a story is told, and chronology, or the temporal arrangement of the events of a story. As the next chapter is devoted to point of view, I shall restrict my observations here to the chronological aspects of discourse – which are order, duration and frequency.

### Order

We tend to recognize the difference between discourse and story most clearly when the events of a novel are not arranged in chronological or linear order, for example Emily Brontë's *Wuthering Heights* or Michael Ondaatje's *The English Patient*. An event that is narrated out of step with the order of the story is called an *anachrony*. There are two types of anachrony – *analepsis* and *prolepsis*.

*   **Analepsis** An analepsis is a flashback or moment of retrospection in a novel. When the narrator of George Eliot's *Middlemarch* discusses the ancestry of the Brooke sisters, this is an analepsis because in the present of the novel these ancestors have long since died.

- **Prolepsis** A prolepsis is a foreshadowing or moment of anticipation in a novel. When Saleem, in Salman Rushdie's *Midnight's Children*, declares at the beginning of the novel that he has no hope of saving his life, this is a prolepsis because he is anticipating his death, which has clearly not happened.

Most prolepses are used to show us the effect of an action before the action itself. For instance, in Toni Morrison's *The Bluest Eye* we are told at the beginning of the novel that Pecola is expecting her father's baby. The rest of the novel relates the events leading up to that point. The reason for this, as in most other novels of this type, is in order to focus our attention on *why* and *how* something happens rather than on *what* happens. In other words, our interest is centred on the process of the story rather than its outcome.

> **Prolepses focus our attention on *why* and *how* something happens rather than on *what* happens.**

Other novels subvert the natural chronology of the story in order to reflect thematic concerns. In Book One of F. Scott Fitzgerald's *Tender is the Night*, for example, we are shown the Divers from Rosemary's point of view at the stage where they have reached 'the exact furthermost evolution of a class'. That is to say, we see the surface success of the Divers when they are the living embodiment of the American Dream. Book Two then goes back in time to show Dick Diver's view of the agonizing route that leads to the apparent success of Book One. Here we find that this success is merely 'a perfect front'. As the linear story of the novel is subverted in this way, we move not chronologically but spatially, first viewing the American Dream from the outside, then moving inside it to see behind the scenes. This spatial progression culminates in Book Three which, in terms of the story, immediately follows Book One. Here, we are taken to the heart of the American Dream, as Nicole Diver's materialism ultimately triumphs over the idealism of Dick.

> **Analepses return us to the origins of an event or character.**

### Duration

Even in the case of novels which follow a natural chronological progression, story and discourse remain distinct, and this is most obvious in terms of the length of time or duration that is spent narrating an event. The discourse of Jonathan Swift's *Gulliver's Travels*, for instance, pursues the same linear course as the story. However, the discourse radically foreshortens its account of the story in some places and dwells at length upon it in other places. For example, the six years Gulliver spends as a ship's surgeon in the West Indies are dispensed with in less than a sentence, whereas his four-year experience in Brobdingnag is told in 80 or so pages. In other words, the story is discursively arranged so as to draw our attention to one event and to minimize our interest in another.

> **Most novels dwell on events of importance and foreshorten the description of unimportant events.**

This is one of the ways in which we, as readers, are compelled by the discourse of a novel to pay careful attention to certain aspects of its story. Typically, the habits and routines of characters are represented metonymically in a few sentences or paragraphs whereas unusual or life-changing experiences are represented at great length. Which is one answer to the age-old question, 'Why do characters never go to the toilet in novels?' – it may be part of the story, but it is not part of the discourse.

### Frequency

Frequency refers to the difference between how many times an event happens in a story and how many times it is narrated at the level of discourse.

- **Singular event** A singular event occurs once and is narrated once. For example, Tom only marries Sophia once in Henry Fielding's *Tom Jones* and it is told only once.
- **Repeated event** A repeated event occurs once in the story but is narrated more than once. For example, the death of the soldier in white only occurs once in the story of Joseph Heller's *Catch-22*, but it is narrated a number of times. Narrating a single event many times helps us to see that event from different points of view, in this case moving from the comic to the sinister to the hysterical.
- **Iterative event** An iterative event occurs many times at the level of story but is narrated only once. For example, the Brangwens grow crops and milk cows many times in D.H. Lawrence's *The Rainbow* but these activities are described in detail only once. Narrating a series of repeated events once is one of the ways in which a narrator represents the kind of routines against which the importance of a singular event can be measured.

### TELOS

Most of the structural features we have been looking at so far involve a relation to the most important part of a novel – the ending. Unlike people, characters in novels move towards a predetermined ending. This predetermined ending is called a *telos*. A *telos* is not just an ending, it is also a goal or aim which culminates the design of the novel. This is because a *telos* makes sense of what went before it, giving meaning and purpose to the rest of the novel.

> **The *telos* is the end *and* aim of the novel – it is what makes sense of the rest of the novel.**

For example, at the end of Iain Banks's novel *The Wasp Factory*, Frank, a boy, finds out that he has been subject to a bizarre gender experiment by his father and that he is really Frances, a girl. This is the *telos* of the novel – it makes sense of what has gone before it, including all 'his' comments about women, such as 'women are a bit too close for comfort as far as I am concerned'. The novel, in other words, has always been moving towards this predefined point or goal. All novels are like this: we only understand the meaning of a novel when it has reached its *telos*.

## WRITING ABOUT STRUCTURE

Every time you write about a novel you should try to include an analysis of its structure. This analysis should always involve an explanation of the effect of the structure on our understanding of the novel. Take a look at this essay extract which tackles the question 'Discuss the theme of secrecy in Joseph Conrad's *The Secret Agent*'.

 *The Secret Agent* is a novel about secrets. All the characters in the novel spy on each other in order to find out each other's secrets. It is even structured around a secret – Stevie's death. Stevie's death is the most important kernel event in the story as it is because of this that Winnie kills Verloc and then kills herself. However, at the level of discourse, the reader never sees it – it is like the centre of one of the empty circles that Stevie keeps drawing. The reason that the reader does not see Stevie's death is to stop us from becoming spies like the rest of the characters in the novel. Spying is compared to pornography and voyeurism by the narrator and so if we saw Stevie's death, the novel's secret, we would become voyeurs too.

This is a good answer for the following reasons:

1  It relates the theme of the novel to its structure, comparing the omission of Stevie's death to the theme of secrecy.
2  It uses the correct technical term to describe the structure where appropriate, in this case the terms 'story', 'discourse' and 'kernel'.
3  It compares the structure to some of the imagery used in the novel, creating a correspondence between Stevie's empty circles and the empty centre of the discourse.
4  It describes the effect of the novel's structure, offering an interpretation of why the novel is constructed around an event that is not narrated.

You will rarely be asked a question solely about the structure of a novel, but you are always expected to include an analysis of it in your answer. If, as in the extract from the essay above, you can offer an explanation of a novel's structure that relates to the themes and imagery of the novel you will significantly improve your grade.

> **You are always expected to write about the structure of a novel.**

### Always ask yourself:

✔  Is this event a kernel or a catalyst and does it have a mimetic or structural cause?
✔  What is the temporal arrangement of the story and how does this arrangement affect our understanding of the novel?
✔  How is the *telos* anticipated by the rest of the novel?

*Point of view simply refers to the angle from which a novel is told. Although it is a concept commonly associated with the novel, all plays and poems are related from a particular perspective too. However, the reason that considerations of point of view are associated with the novel is that the novel form allows for the most complex constructions of point of view. Nevertheless, all of these complex constructions always begin with two simple questions: Who speaks? Where are they speaking from?*

## NARRATORS

The point of view which dominates most novels is the one belonging to its narrator. A narrator is simply whoever is telling the story. The narrator is not necessarily the author and you should never confuse the two. Indeed, unless you are explicitly asked to mention them, authors (and particularly their 'intentions') should be left out of your essays completely.

Narrators can be classified according to where they are telling the story from. In narratology, which is the study of narratives, 'diegesis' is the technical term for 'story' and 'diegetic' is the adjectival form of the word. The three levels of narrator are:

1  **Extradiegetic** An extradiegetic narrator is a narrator who operates above or outside the story he or she is telling.. For example, the narrator of George Eliot's *Middlemarch* is extradiegetic, as is the narrator of Henry Fielding's *Tom Jones*.
2  **Intradiegetic** An intradiegetic narrator is a narrator who participates in the story, or diegesis, told by an extradiegetic narrator. For example, Frankenstein, in Mary Shelley's *Frankenstein*, tells a story within the story told by Robert Walton. Similarly, Marlow, in Joseph Conrad's *Lord Jim*, tells a story within the story told by the anonymous extradiegetic narrator.
3  **Hypodiegetic** A hypodiegetic narrator is a narrator who tells a story within a story within a story. Although many novels include discrete examples of this type of narrator, it is rarer to find it in extended use. One notable example, though, is Henry James's *The Turn of the Screw* in which the anonymous 'I' is the extradiegetic narrator, Douglas is the intradiegetic narrator and the governess is the hypodiegetic narrator.

Narrators can also be classified according to whether or not they participate in the story they are narrating.

1  **Heterodiegetic** A narrator who does not take part in the story he or she is narrating is a heterodiegetic narrator. The narrator of D.H. Lawrence's *Sons and Lovers* is heterodiegetic, as is the narrator of Jane Austen's *Pride and Prejudice*.

2  **Homodiegetic** A narrator who participates in the story he or she is narrating is a homodiegetic narrator. Saleem Sinai is the homodiegetic narrator of Salman Rushdie's *Midnight's Children*. Lemuel Gulliver is the homodiegetic narrator of Jonathan Swift's *Gulliver's Travels*.

If a narrator is both extradiegetic and heterodiegetic, then that narrator is usually called an omniscient or all-knowing narrator. An omniscient narrator is a narrator who has an unlimited perspective, knowing everything that has happened and will happen, and what every character thinks and does. Homodiegetic narrators, on the other hand, tend to have a restricted knowledge of the actions and thoughts of the other characters in the story. This is called a limited point of view.

> **Narrators that know everything have an omniscient point of view, whereas narrators that know only some things have a limited point of view.**

Exceptions to this rule are novels where homodiegetic narrators are also heterodiegetic. This can occur, for example, when adults narrate the story of their childhood, such as David and Pip in Charles Dickens's *David Copperfield* and *Great Expectations* respectively. In these cases, the homodiegetic narrators are blessed with the benefit of hindsight and therefore function effectively in the same way as traditional extradiegetic narrators.

## WHAT DO I DO WITH THESE CLASSIFICATIONS?

If you can identify and name the type of narrator in the novel you are writing about with technical accuracy you will be suitably rewarded by the grade you get for your essay. However, if you just leave it there then you will have left your essay at the level of description. Once you have identified a particular point of view, you next need to analyse its effects upon your understanding of the text.

> **Always analyse what effect is achieved by using a specific type of narrator.**

For example, Nick Carraway is the homodiegetic narrator of F. Scott Fitzgerald's *The Great Gatsby*. He goes out of his way in the first few pages of the novel to assure us that he is a fundamentally decent and reliable character. In doing so, he assumes the qualities we tend to associate with conventional heterodiegetic narrators – those of objectivity, impartiality and omniscience. We therefore tend to read the novel as if it were narrated from a quite different point of view than the one it actually is written from.

However, if we examine Nick's narration as we would most homodiegetic narration, that is in terms of having a vested interest and a limited point of view, it transpires that Nick is actually quite an unreliable narrator. To take just one aspect of his unreliability, we quickly find that Nick has a very active imagination. He constantly invents conversations, for example, making up dialogue for his father, the butler and even, at one stage, for the corpse of Gatsby. This tactic is emblematic of Nick's practice throughout the novel of speaking for Gatsby, of ventriloquizing his thoughts *as if* they really were Gatsby's own. Phrases like 'as if' and 'as though' are smuggled into the narrative by Nick on almost every other page. They are the overt signs of a covert project to understand Gatsby as a great deal more than just Gatsby; to understand Gatsby, that is, as he is refashioned by Nick's imagination from gangster to romantic idol. The reason that Nick is largely successful in doing this, at least on a first reading of the novel, is that he feigns the attributes of a heterodiegetic narrator while in fact being a homodiegetic narrator.

> **Some narrators are unreliable and you have to analyse their influence on your understanding of a novel.**

## POLYPHONY

Although the narrator is usually the controlling and dominant voice in a novel, it is not normally the only one. Indeed, most novels are composed of a number of different voices, all interacting with each other. This interaction is called *polyphony*. Polyphony in novels can take many forms, but the three most prominent are:

1 **Free indirect discourse** Free indirect discourse is a means of representing speech which is midway between direct and indirect discourse. *Direct discourse* is a quotation of dialogue, for example: 'Stuart said, "Sure I've got to do it"'. *Indirect discourse* is a summary of dialogue, for example: 'Stuart told him he had to do it'. *Free indirect discourse* is half quotation and half summary, for example: 'Sure he had to do it'. Speech is often represented in different ways, rather than solely by one means. For example, the first of the following two sentences from Gustave Flaubert's *Madame Bovary* is indirect discourse and the second is free indirect discourse: 'The clerk declared that idealistic natures were not easily understood. *He* had fallen in love with her at first sight.' As can be seen here, free indirect discourse combines the voice of the narrator with that of a character. It is essentially the narrator invading or mimicking the voice of a character, often in order to create an ironic effect or to influence the affections of the reader.

2 **Internal focalization** If free indirect discourse signifies the invasion of a character's voice by the narrator, then internal focalization is the invasion of the narrator's voice by a character's voice. This is not necessarily a matter of dialogue, but often of colouring or slanting a description in terms of the temperament or outlook of a character. For example, when the narrator of *Madame Bovary* declares that 'The next day went, oh, so slowly!', this is not a neutral description of a day, which of course always goes at the same speed from an objective point of view. Rather, the speed of the day is described from Emma Bovary's point of view. In other words, the narrator describes the day *as if* he or she were Emma.

3   **Intertextuality** If the voices within a novel are often hybrids, quoting, mimicking and ventriloquizing each other, it is also the case that these voices can quote, mimic and ventriloquize voices from outside of the novel. This is called *intertextuality*. It can occur at a local level or more generally within a novel. For example, the characterization of Gradgrind, in Charles Dickens's *Hard Times*, draws upon the intertext of the philosophy of utilitarianism that was coming to dominate public discourse in mid-nineteenth century Britain. His repeated injunction to give him the facts is a satirized mimicking of that discourse. At a more general level, Jean Rhys's *Wide Sargasso Sea* uses Charlotte Brontë's *Jane Eyre* as the pretext for the whole novel, taking one character, the infamous madwoman in the attic, and weaving a new story around her. By doing this, Rhys manages to open up themes that were unexplored in the original intertext, thereby creating a new point of view about Brontë's novel. This is typical of the effects of all polyphony. By juxtaposing different voices in dialogue with each other, novels foster the creation of original points of view.

## PARTIALITY

If we have seen so far that point of view is determined by the knowledge of the narrator (across both time and space) and by the competing voices of a novel, it is also worth bearing in mind that point of view is a question of partiality. No text is ever purely disinterested. It will always be prejudiced in favour of one character over another, one idea over another. At its weakest a novel's point of view is a matter of bias; at its strongest a novel's point of view is a matter of ideology. Your job when you analyse a text is to determine the point of view from which a story is told and to demonstrate what effect this perspective has on our understanding of the story.

> **Every novel is told from a point of view and every point of view displays a form of partiality.**

All of Charles Dickens's novels, for example, tend to sentimentalize children. Dickens's children are, on the whole, innocent waifs and angels put upon by a corrupt society. This fact, in itself, betrays a certain point of view. However, it is certainly not a child's point of view, because children do not sentimentalize themselves. It is therefore clearly the point of view of a mature adult who has long forgotten what it means to be a child.

Some authors, such as Ernest Hemingway, try to eliminate the partiality of a point of view completely. His short story 'Hills Like White Elephants', for example, depicts a man trying to persuade a woman to have an operation although, crucially, we are never told what that operation is. Written almost entirely in the indicative mood, there is very little extradiegetic narration and what there is employs denotative diction and a minimal amount of figurative language. The story largely consists of dialogue concerning a pronoun – 'it' – about which we are never fully enlightened. In other words, there appears to be no point of view; the story is merely a disinterested observation.

> **Some authors try to eliminate partiality from a novel's point of view: this is impossible.**

However, when we read the story we, as readers, supply the missing point of view. We do this by making an assumption about the nature of the operation. Some readers think that it – the operation – is an abortion, while other think that it concerns having a tooth out. Whichever assumption we make alters the way in which we look at the characters. If it is an abortion, we might think that the man is trying unduly to pressurize the woman. If we think it is having a tooth out, we might consider the man's persuasive tactics to be in the woman's best interest. Whatever we decide creates a point of view, a bias or a prejudice. As the story's narration tries to be disinterested, we might conclude that it mimics the man's feigned objectivity as he persuades the woman to have the operation. In other words, the point of view of the story is the same as the man's point of view. Both are seemingly impartial but this very impartiality conceals a hidden agenda.

## WRITING ABOUT POINT OF VIEW

As I mentioned in the previous chapter, point of view is part of the discourse of a novel rather than the story. Your job when analysing a novel is to show how this affects our understanding of the story. Take a look at the following extract from an essay answering the question 'What is the role of irony in Henry James's *Washington Square?'*

 One of the most interesting aspects of *Washington Square* is the point of view of the narrator. The narrator is a third-person, omniscient narrator, both extradiegetic and heterodiegetic. This might make you think the narrator is impartial, treating all characters in the same way because he or she is above the action. However, the ironic tone of the narrator is the same as that used by Dr Sloper. The narrator therefore sides with Sloper, until, that is, Sloper dies. The narrator then stops being ironic and adopts the non-ironic tone of Catherine instead, displaying a bias in her favour which ultimately concludes the novel.

This is a good answer for the following reasons:

1   It describes the point of view of the narrator using the correct technical terms.
2   It analyses the effect of the point of view, demonstrating how it creates a bias in favour of a particular character.
3   It examines the way in which the narrator's point of view changes and develops during the course of the novel.

As you can see above, this question does not explicitly ask for an analysis of the novel's point of view. Nevertheless, a good essay always considers how a novel's point of view affects our comprehension of the novel's story.

### Always ask yourself:
✔   What type of narrator is this and what effect does this have?
✔   What forms of polyphony are in the novel and what effects do these have?
✔   What effects do the knowledge and prejudices of the narrator have on our understanding of the novel?

*One of the main aspects of a text about which you will be asked to write is character. Questions such as, 'Discuss the character of the Dog-Woman in Jeanette Winterson's* Sexing the Cherry', *or, 'Compare and contrast the characters of Casaubon and Lydgate in George Eliot's* Middlemarch', *are, unfortunately, all too common. I say 'unfortunately' because questions such as these are, in fact, traps for the unwary student. What you are really being asked to analyse in such questions is not character, but characterization.*

## THE DIFFERENCE BETWEEN CHARACTER AND CHARACTERIZATION

The difference between character and characterization is relatively straightforward:

- **A character is a representation of a person.** If you are writing about character, you are merely describing the combination of attributes and traits that distinguish a particular individual. So, for example, you might describe the character of Dr Sloper in Henry James's *Washington Square* as cruel, domineering and sarcastic.

- **Characterization, on the other hand, is the means used to create a character or representation of a person.** The trick here is to think of character as an effect. Your job when you are writing about character is to show how that effect is produced. So, if you think that Dr Sloper is cruel, domineering and sarcastic, you need to prove how that impression or effect is produced. In this case, you might wish to refer not only to his own actions, but also to the way in which the other characters in the novel think of him or react to him.

The distinction between character and characterization is vital to bear in mind. This is because if you think of characters in novels as merely characters, rather than as the effects of characterization, then you are more likely to fall into one of the biggest traps in essay writing: treating the characters as if they were real people. The problem with this is two-fold. First, it lulls students into speculating about the characters, attributing motives to them for which there is no proof or conjecturing on how happily they lived after the end of the novel. Secondly, when students discuss characters as if they were people, the tendency is for them merely to *describe* the different traits of a particular individual, when what they should be doing if they wish to get a high grade is *analysing* how these traits are conveyed by the text in question.

> **Never speculate about characters in novels or treat them as if they were real people.**

So, for example, if you were asked to discuss the Cheeryble Brothers in Charles Dickens's *Nicholas Nickleby* you would not merely content yourself with stating that they are kind and jolly. You would, rather, go on to point out how this is conveyed (as with most of Dickens's characters) by means of a physical correspondence in which the generous (or, frankly, obese) proportions of the two men are symbols of their generosity of conduct, and their twinkling eyes and rosy cheeks are stock ways of representing good-humoured characters. Indeed, if you had read Chapter 12 of this book, you might then go on to show how the Cheerybles are represented metonymically by their big bellies, twinkling eyes and rosy cheeks – that is, how these individual physical characteristics are used to represent them as a whole when they are described.

Not resting there, you might then analyse their highly suggestive name – Cheeryble – and propose that it is an *aptronym*. An aptronym is a name that affords an insight into or hint about the personality or purpose of a character. In this case, 'Cheeryble' helps to convey the congenial temperament of the two men. From there, you might wish to demonstrate that character is usually an effect of repetition and that we would not refer to the Cheerybles as 'kind' if they only undertook a single act of charity and spent the rest of their time evicting poor people from their large selection of properties.

> **An aptronym is a name that suggests something about the personality or purpose of a character.**

## SHOWING AND TELLING

In terms of generalizing about methods of characterization, one of the most useful distinctions you can make is between 'showing' and 'telling'.

- **Showing**  If a novel *shows* you what a character does, you are then able to infer for yourself the personality of that character.
- **Telling**  If a novel *tells* you what a character is like, then you do not have to infer anything about the personality of the character.

All of which seems fairly straightforward, but there are a couple of points you have to bear in mind about this distinction:

1  The difference between showing and telling is to a large extent a matter of how much the narrator intrudes upon the depiction of the characters. Telling involves commenting on a character's actions or thoughts, whereas showing does not. However, it is worthwhile remembering that characters are never purely 'shown'; they do not exist independently of the narrator who, in fact, controls what is shown and how it is shown. There is no purely objective or neutral way of describing an action.

2  As there is no objective way of describing a story, what the distinction between showing and telling reveals is that narrators are characters too. They are usually not named or described and usually do not take part in the story,

but all narrators are prejudiced, which is to say that like characters they have a subjective vision of the world, or, more specifically, of the novel they are in. In order to own up to this fact, some novels, such as Joseph Conrad's *Heart of Darkness* or F. Scott Fitzgerald's *The Great Gatsby*, turn their narrators into overt characters, such as Marlow or Nick Carraway. In these novels, the interest lies in the difference between what the narrator tells you and what the narrator shows you. So, for example, Marlow *tells* you that Kurtz is a remarkable human being, but he *shows* you that Kurtz is a cannibal with scant regard for anyone. In this sense, the distinction between showing and telling discloses more about the character of the narrator than the characters in the novel.

## THE FIVE METHODS OF CHARACTERIZATION

Broadly speaking, there are five main methods of characterization, or of creating characters, in novels:

1 Through what characters say
2 Through what characters think
3 Through what characters do
4 Through how characters are described
5 Through the reactions of other characters.

**1 What characters say.** Well-drawn characters usually have distinctive styles of speech. This distinctiveness may be a matter of register or tone, such as Marlow in Joseph Conrad's *Heart of Darkness*, whose tone is distinctly dark and lugubrious. It may be a matter of subject matter, such as Emma's obsession with match-making in Jane Austen's *Emma*. Or it may be a matter of diction, such as Mr Micawber's absurd use of a hundred words where three would do in Charles Dickens's *David Copperfield*.

In each case, the point of this is not only to provide the reader with an insight into the personality of the characters involved, but also to distinguish them from the rest of the characters in the novel. One of the reasons for the development of the novel as a form is to enable the most intimate articulation of character. As dialogue is an interactive mode of characterization, it is something of a proofing ground for the distinctiveness of a character. For example, Okonkwo in Chinua Achebe's *Things Fall Apart* is distinguished in what he says precisely because he fails to employ the proverbial speech which everyone else does in the Igbo community. This not only marks him out as a character, showing him to be an individual, but also foreshadows the break-up of the community following their colonization by the Europeans, who advocate an individualist society.

**2 What characters think.** The great advantage of novels is that we are given access to characters' thoughts. In terms of building characterization, the most important feature of this inner access is how it contrasts with what a character says or does. This is because a character's thoughts are the most secret part of that character's identity – they are hidden from all the other characters in the novel and only the reader has access to them. So, for example, we know that Madame Bovary, in the novel of the same name by Gustave Flaubert, is prone to infidelity long before her husband does because we can see from her thoughts that she is dissatisfied with the petty provincial life he forces her to lead.

**3   What characters do.** Most characters begin a novel bound to routine. It is against this background of habit and custom that a single action can either indicate the development of a character or, at the very least, confirm the importance of a latent characteristic. When Carlo, for example, in Louis de Bernières' *Captain Corelli's Mandolin*, places himself in front of Corelli before the firing squad it confirms that his love for Corelli is as altruistic as his final letter suggests it is. Equally, when Thomas Gradgrind betrays Stephen Blackpool in Charles Dickens's *Hard Times*, it confirms his twisted development and gives the lie to the pious dialogue he exchanges with his sister.

**4   How characters are described.** The appearance, or an aspect of the appearance of a character is very often used to throw light on that character's personality. For example, in Toni Morrison's *Beloved*, Sethe has 'a tree' on her back created by the scars she received from being whipped. The deliberate description of these scars as 'a tree' by Sethe draws attention to them. It feeds in not only to the motif of the tree in the rest of novel but also in to the symbolic value of trees in world culture, from the Tree of Knowledge, Yggdrasil and the Bo-Tree, to the common symbolism of trees in terms of genealogy, roots and history generally. In doing this, the tree on Sethe's back helps us to understand her character better, for her character and its development in the novel are predicated upon her relationship to a personal and public history – the history of slavery.

We can see, then, that the 'tree' is literally behind her, she has her back to it in the same way that she has turned her back on the traumatic memories of the past. She cannot feel it, yet it is a part of her. It is the result of what someone else has done to her and she requires someone else to tell her what it is and to decipher its significance for her. In this way, the 'tree' on Sethe's back becomes a potent symbol of her struggle to deal with the past. And because the tree is used as a symbol in other contexts throughout the novel and because it has a common currency beyond *Beloved*, Sethe's 'tree' also compels us to interpret Sethe as a character representative of the millions of others who suffered in slavery.

**5   The reactions of other characters.** The way in which characters react to each other is also an important method of characterization. For example, in Joseph Conrad's *Heart of Darkness* we can see how the character of Kurtz is made up almost exclusively of the reactions of Marlow and the other cameo characters in the novel. Indeed, much of the material on Kurtz reaches the reader by way of third- or even fourth-hand hearsay. Kurtz's character is thus largely an effect of rumour. Even when Kurtz does finally speak, much of what he says, such as the infamous ' "The Horror! The Horror!" ', is somewhat inscrutable. The reason for this is that Kurtz represents the 'heart of darkness' and to illuminate him more clearly would have been to render him, figuratively speaking, as lightness rather than darkness.

## REPETITION, CONFLICT AND DEVELOPMENT IN CHARACTERIZATION

The key to all these different methods of characterization is the relationship between repetition and conflict. A character is established largely through the repetition of what she or he says, thinks, does and how that character is described and provokes reactions. In a leading character, however, there is usually an internal conflict which threatens and ultimately breaks that pattern of repetition. This marks the development of the character.

> **A character is established through repetition; a character changes through the resolution of a conflict.**

So, for example, Catherine Sloper in Henry James's *Washington Square* is initially established in the novel as an ingenuous, dutiful daughter by the repetition of acts and thoughts of deference to her father. However, she soon finds herself torn by a conflict between the love for her father and the love for her suitor. This conflict is resolved when she finally refuses to obey her father's injunction not to marry her suitor. This decision marks her development as a character because in making it she changes from a dutiful daughter to a woman of independent thought.

The novelist E.M. Forster advanced a useful distinction between characters that develop and those that do not. Characters that do not develop he called flat characters. A flat character is merely an effect of repetition and never changes. Charles Dickens's novels are populated by dozens of these characters. They are often created through the iteration of a catch-phrase such as Uriah Heep's perpetual reminder that he is 'humble' in *David Copperfield*. A round character, on the other hand, is one that develops or changes in the course of the novel. Elizabeth Bennet, for example, in Jane

> **Flat characters do not develop, whereas round characters change in the course of a novel.**

Austen's *Pride and Prejudice*, develops as a character when she overcomes her prejudice towards Darcy, he having overcome his condescending pride towards her.

### Always ask yourself:
✔ Am I analysing the character or the characterization?
✔ What are the methods of characterization that the novel uses and what effects do they have?
✔ Does the character develop, and if so, how is that development realized?

*The novel is the young upstart of literature. Although certain novel-istic practices are thousands of years old, the novel as we recognize it has only been in existence for about three hundred years. Since then it has wasted little time in becoming the most popular and most examined form of literature, easily outstripping the more estab-lished genres of poetry and drama. One of the reasons for this appeal is the chameleon-like quality of the novel or the ways it has changed over time. In order to help you contextualize your analyses of a particular novel, then, this chapter will examine the broad changes that have taken place within the genre.*

## DEVELOPMENT OF THE NOVEL

Of the forms of writing from which the novel developed, probably the most impor-tant is the romance. Originating in twelfth-century France, romances are long fictions dealing with chivalry and courtly love. While the French romances tend to feature the exploits of Charlemagne, many of the English romances, such as Thomas Malory's *Le Morte d'Arthur*, deal with the adventures of King Arthur and the knights of the Round Table. These fantastic and magical tales were originally written mainly in verse, but over time prose became the most popular format.

> **The novel developed out of romances which were fictions dealing with love and chivalry.**

During the seventeenth century the subject matter of romances became a popular source of satire in plays, such as Francis Beaumont and John Fletcher's *The Knights of the Burning Pestle*, and prose works, such as Miguel de Cervantes's *Don Quixote*. Over the next one hundred years or so such attacks on romances helped to create a distinction between romances and novels (a word which derives from the Latin for 'new story') based upon a difference in subject matter. Whereas romances dealt with the fantastic and the legendary, novels featured more realistic and probable stories.

The success of the new novel format, including work by such authors as Henry Fielding, Daniel Defoe and Samuel Richardson, was not just due to subject matter. It was also dependent on several other factors, including *increasing literacy, tech-nological advances* and *the advent of capitalism*.

- **Increasing literacy** In 1600 only a quarter of the male population of England was literate but by the mid nineteenth century the literacy rate was closer to three quarters of all men. This had a great effect on the popularity of novels because whereas poetry and drama were oral-based media, novels were predominantly a print medium which required the skill of reading.

- **Technological advances** Another vital factor in the growth in popularity of the novel was the development of printing technologies. Increases in paper production and the introduction of copyright laws also helped to unleash the power of the printing presses, turning what had once been a restricted consumption of literature into a mass market.
- **The advent of capitalism** From the sixteenth century onwards feudalism began to wither in the face of the kind of market-based economy we now know as capitalism. Writers were no longer dependent on patronage and subscriptions for their income and could appeal directly to the newly enriched middle classes instead. Indeed, the novel was particularly appealing to the new capitalist class because it depicted the very individualism upon which the market is based. Under feudalism people were defined by their place or role in the order of things. Under capitalism this stratified community gave way to a belief that people were able to define their own role and ultimately their own characters. This individualism manifested itself most markedly in the increasing distinction between private and public lives, a distinction which the novel alone was capable of fully articulating with its techniques of focalization and narrative voices. In addition to these techniques, the experience of reading a novel was itself private. This was because you could (and still can) pick it up and put it down at your own convenience and because reading a novel depends on the development of a voice in an individual's mind, rather than on hearing the voices of others.

> **Novels tend to be written by, read by, and be about individuals.**

## TYPES OF NOVEL

There are generally two ways of conceptualizing novels, either historically or generically. In other words, the novel can be studied either in terms of its historical development or in terms of techniques and subject matter which cut across historical boundaries. There is also a third way, which I will undertake here, which understands the differences in techniques and subject matter as determined in large part by history. These differences are broadly referred to by the terms *realism*, *modernism* and *postmodernism*.

### Realism

As plain as the nose on your face and as hard to see without going cross-eyed, realism is notoriously difficult to define. At the level of common sense it refers to those novels which depict real life, such as Jane Austen's *Pride and Prejudice*. This definition of realism therefore seems fairly straightforward until we remember that real life is not just made up of things but thoughts and feelings as well. If you have a secret and intense affection for someone called Karl or Emma, no one can see it but it is undeniably real to you. Similarly, a farmyard full of talking pigs is unrealistic in the sense that you never see one, but if they are in George Orwell's *Animal Farm* then the ideas they talk about are real in the sense that they relate to the issues of the world we inhabit.

> **Realism refers not only to novels that depict life but also to novels that depict issues that are part of life, even if the depiction is unrealistic.**

With this problem in mind, it is perhaps useful to recall that the novel developed out of a distinction between it and romances. The novel defined itself against romances by depicting scenes and characters that its readership might find by looking out of the window. Early novels are therefore realist. Indeed, novels generally not only remained realist until the end of the nineteenth century, they attempted to achieve greater and greater levels of realism. Novels did this both by minimizing those features, such as intrusive narrators, which reminded people they were actually reading works of fiction, and by concentrating more and more on the mundane aspects of life, such as working and marriage, rather than adventures or extravagant exploits. When you describe a

> **Most novels written before the twentieth century are realist.**

novel as realist, then, make sure you explain exactly what you take this to mean, be it a way of referring to a depiction of recognizable scenes, a way of depicting recognizable ideas, or a way of minimizing the fictional aspect of a text.

## Modernism

If the novel was broadly realist from its birth to the end of the nineteenth century, it was broadly modernist till the 1950s. When I say 'broadly' I am really only referring to the novels considered important by academic critics, because on the whole the novel is *still* realist in terms of the kind of novels that most people read. This is because modernism marks the point where novels began to explore their own private lives, as it were, turning in on themselves and exploring fictional techniques which many people cannot relate to in the same way they can a realist depiction of life. The most famous of these techniques is the stream of consciousness where a narrative is given over to the random thoughts and feelings of a character, which can be found in works like Virginia Woolf's *To the Lighthouse* and James Joyce's *Ulysses*. This technique exemplifies another aspect of modernism, which is its concern with depicting the subjective

> **Modernist novels depict life as the characters experience it rather than showing the objective experience of a character's life.**

world of individuals, showing life as characters experience it rather than showing the objective experience of a character's life, which is what realism did.

## Postmodernism

The novel has been broadly postmodernist since the 1960s. If the passage from realism to modernism was marked by an ever more intense focus on the individual and a subjective experience of the world, postmodernism signals an end to this trend and a return to objectivity. This return takes many forms. Some novels, such as Kurt Vonnegut's *Slaughterhouse-Five*, depict utterly flat characters, devoid of the idiosyncrasies which we understand as forming characters in the first place, and instead being more like the stock or stereotypical characters of romances or medieval drama. On the other hand, a novel like Toni Morrison's *Beloved* has highly developed characters but it does not show their consciousness, for example Sethe's, swallowing up the world in the way that Bloom's does in *Ulysses*. Instead it shows the way in which the world erupts into Sethe's consciousness.

> **Postmodernist novels signal the end of the introspective trend of realism and modernism.**

Like modernism, postmodernism is also concerned with exploring the techniques of fiction. However, unlike modernism, postmodernism does not employ these techniques in order to imitate consciousness more realistically or to portray a subjective world more precisely. Rather, it tends to use such methods to remind people of the fictional nature of the novels they are reading and also of the fictional construction of the world. These fictions about fictions, called metafictions or self-reflexive novels, are the 'real' antithesis of realism, for instead of suppressing all signs of the writing process they draw attention to it, and

> **A metafiction is a novel which displays its own fictional qualities.**

even, in the case of John Fowles's *The French Lieutenant's Woman*, have the author turn up as a character amidst the more traditional fictional characters.

### WRITING ABOUT THE NOVEL

The history of the novel, then, represents a journey into and out of the realistic depiction of the private lives of individuals. The three terms – realism, modernism and postmodernism – represent subtle shifts in emphasis on that journey. When you write about a novel you do not necessarily have to use these terms to describe it, but you should maintain an awareness of the issues these terms represent and try to inscribe that awareness within your approach to a text.

> **The history of the novel represents a journey into and out of the realistic depiction of the private lives of individuals.**

### Always ask yourself:

✔ In what ways is the novel realist, modernist or postmodernist?

✔ Does the novel try to depict life realistically or does it draw attention to its own fictional status?

✔ Do the individual characters in the novel impose their consciousness on the world or does the world impose upon them?

# Analysing gothic, historiographic and postcolonial novels

*There are many different subgenres of the novel, such as science-fiction, detective novels and romances, which we all recognize. In recent years three particular types of subgenre have come to prominence both generally and on the exam syllabuses; they are gothic, historiographic and postcolonial novels. In order to help you analyse these three subgenres, this chapter will explain the themes they explore and what features to look for when you read and write about them.*

## THE GOTHIC, THE HISTORIOGRAPHIC AND THE POSTCOLONIAL

The prevalence of these types of novel indicates a contemporary concern with their subject matter – that is, with the gothic, the historiographic and the postcolonial. So although the novels in this chapter are devoted to these subjects, other novels use elements of their techniques and themes. When you write about other types of novel, then, you should not be afraid to contextualize them in terms of these novels, showing how and in what ways they exhibit the influence of the gothic, the historiographic and the postcolonial.

> **You can identify elements of the gothic, the historiographic and the postcolonial in other novels.**

## Gothic novels

*Who are the chief exponents?*
Gothic novels have been an identifiable genre for almost 250 years, becoming more and less fashionable in waves of popularity. The most prominent authors are Angela Carter, Ann Radcliffe, Edgar Allen Poe (for his short stories), Mary Shelley, Bram Stoker and Horace Walpole.

*What does 'gothic' mean?*
Gothic novels developed out of the genre of romance in the late eighteenth century (see Chapter 29) and like 'romance', 'gothic' was a pejorative term used to signify an interest in the Middle Ages, with all its associations of superstition, magic and primitive customs. In this sense, the term was used as a way of setting off the past from the culture and civilization of the present. It represented the barbarity that humankind had overcome to produce the age of enlightenment. Even today 'gothic' still resonates with some of this meaning, representing the part of our culture which is an excess or a surplus, above and beyond the rational.

> **Gothic novels represent that part of our culture which is an excess or a surplus, above and beyond the rational.**

*What are the most common techniques in gothic novels?*
It is partly the adjective that makes a novel gothic, for in gothic novels a castle is never simply a castle, it is always a *decaying* castle, vaults are *labyrinthine*, mountains are *jagged* and everything is always *dark* and *gloomy*. Gothic novels therefore tend to use the rhetorical figure called the 'pleonasm'. A pleonasm is an excessive use of words. Gothic novels are often pleonastic in that they spend so much of the narrative describing the atmosphere, piling up the adjectives and adverbs and the figures of speech in order to make it more and more ominous, mysterious and frightening.

*What are the most common themes of gothic novels?*
The main theme of gothic novels is the irrational. This relates not only to what cannot be explained by scientific reasoning but also to what is produced by an excess of scientific reasoning, such as when a man assumes the position of God in Mary Shelley's *Frankenstein*. Gothic themes therefore tend to centre upon those parts of our culture which our culture has to exclude in order to make sense of itself – such as ghosts, madness, terror and even nature.

*What is an archetypal gothic novel?*
Horace Walpole's *The Castle of Otranto*.

**Historiographic novels**

*Who are the chief exponents?*
There are dozens and dozens of historiographic novelists, as historiography has become a major concern over the past thirty years, but some of the ones you are most likely to encounter include Peter Ackroyd, Margaret Atwood, Gabriel García Márquez, Michael Ondaatje, Salman Rushdie and Graham Swift.

*What does 'historiographic' mean?*
'Historiographic' means 'writing about history writing'. A conventional historical novel writes about an event or series of events intertwined with fictional characters, whereas an historiographic novel might write about the same event but will also reflect on itself and consider the problems of writing about history.

> **Historiographic novels examine the difficulty of writing about history.**

*What are the most common techniques in historiographic novels?*
Historiographic novels commonly use competing points of view in order to undermine any stable notion of the story they are telling. One of the more popular ways of doing this is to include competing sets of 'fake' documentation in the novel. They

also tend to employ intrusive narrators so as to emphasize the subjective character of the history.

*What are the most common themes of historiographic novels?*
History is clearly the major theme of these novels, but more specifically they tend to question (without necessarily answering) the objective and subjective nature of history. They tend to stress the narrative qualities of history, and therefore its fictitiousness, but in so doing they question the possibility of writing a history which is faithful to the period they are writing about, rather than just being a mirror of the present.

*What is an archetypal historiographic novel?*
Graham Swift's *Waterland*.

## Postcolonial novels

*Who are the chief exponents?*
Postcolonialist novelists are mainly twentieth-century writers, such as Chinua Achebe, V.S. Naipaul, Jean Rhys, Salman Rushdie and Ngũgĩ Wa Thiong'o. They mainly write about those countries which were colonies of the European empires.

*What does 'postcolonial' mean?*
Novelists are described as 'postcolonial' in order to indicate that they are writing about countries *after* the defeat of the empires that colonized them. Some critics think that this title also suggests that the effects of colonialism have disappeared when they have patently not. These critics prefer to use the term 'neo-colonial'. This refers to the effects of colonialism, implying that they are still on-going and in competition with a country's native culture.

> **Postcolonial novels examine the effects of colonialism.**

*What are the most common techniques in postcolonial novels?*
The most common technique, although it is not necessarily a technique by choice, is the use of a doubled or hybrid voice. A hybrid voice is one that reflects elements of both the indigenous culture of the writer and the culture that colonized it.

*What are the most common themes of postcolonial novels?*
Postcolonial novels engage in a double project – both trying to unearth and reinvigorate their own national cultures, and showing the effects of colonialism on those cultures. Writers who address a specifically European readership also try to demystify the stereotypical images of colonized peoples in European novels. By not showing these peoples as exotic, instinctive, racially motivated and collectively self-consistent, but rather as individuals with their own sense of culture and civility, they also force Europeans to concede the partiality of their own experience.

*What is an archetypal postcolonial novel?*

Chinua Achebe's *Things Fall Apart.*

**Always ask yourself:**
- ✔ What techniques and themes make this a gothic novel?
- ✔ What techniques and themes make this a historiographic novel?
- ✔ What techniques and themes make this a postcolonial novel?

# Index